Healing

Selections from the Sermons of Fr Phil Wolfe,
Revised Edition

Compiled and Edited by Our Lady of Sorrows Press

2026

First Edition published in 2018

Cover photo at Shrine of Our Lady of Good Help. Used with permission.
Book and Cover design by Our Lady of Sorrows Press.

ISBN: 978-1-7328029-2-6

Revised Edition: February 2, 2026

Dedicated to Our Lady of Fatima

and for all those who start on the healing journey...

the editor

Table of Contents

FOREWORD

Except from Original Sin, we all have different wounds. Our different wounds either remain a painful remembrance or transform us into the charity of Jesus Christ. For example, my own wounds of my childhood caused me to shirk away from English class and public speaking. The devil knows what weapons God has placed in our soul that will be used to attack his kingdom of darkness. The devil tempted me to fear English and public speaking. But by the work of healing, I was able to overcome those temptations, although it took a long time. It is our lot in this life to allow Jesus and the Blessed Virgin Mary to transform our wounds into weapons to extend the kingdom of God. My wounds of fear of English and public speaking have been transformed by Jesus and Mary and now I am an author of several books about my mission, devotion to the Holy Face, and books on prayer. Being asked to write books has led me to be a missionary on the devotion to the Holy Face of Jesus as it is found in the Archconfraternity of the Holy Face. This has allowed me to enjoy flying around the world to speak in thirty of fifty states in the USA at the time of this writing, and there are engagements around the world scheduled in the future. It is a joy to be used as an instrument of God to spread a devotion that was given to us by Jesus to convert revolutionary men. St. Paul said, "Who now rejoice in my sufferings for you, and fill up those things that are wanting in the sufferings of Christ, in my flesh, for his body, which is the church" (I Col. i, 24.)

Fr. Wolfe is being used by God as an instrument to help people realize that wounds are alright and that Jesus wants us to open them up to Him and invite Him into our woundedness so that they can be transformed, healed and even be used to extend the glory of God. I know of at least one priest and several other people that God has used Fr. Wolfe to heal when they thought it was impossible. I hope that this book will open up people's wounds and that they will find healing in his easy steps:

1. It is not necessary to call wounds to mind if it hurts too much at first. This can be done later when the healing makes us stronger.

2. Sometimes Our Lady needs to be asked to go behind the walls of our wounds if we can't handle even to think of them. She will do her work once we ask her.

3. Some people have a problem when they think of the Jesus Christ the Man. They need to think of the babe held in the arms of the Blessed Virgin Mary.

4. When we are ready to be healed, we need to pick one wound at a time. It may hurt and that is because pain is going out. The time of the wound is when pain went in.

5. Forgiveness is a necessary ingredient.

6. Formal renunciations are needed to be made to release the disordered attachment to the wound.

7. Persistence is required to release the pain from wounds.

8. One knows that he is getting healed when the recalling the event which caused the wound is less painful.

9. A spiritual scar can now be used to extend the Kingdom of God and cooperate with the redemption of Jesus Christ and the reign of the Blessed Virgin Mary. (This is when the soul begins to live heaven now.)

This all makes sense because Catholics are taught to meditate on the wounds of Jesus. Remember when St. Thomas the Apostle doubted the Resurrection? Jesus came to him and told him to put his hands in His wounds. Jesus used His wounds to convince St. Thomas that He rose from the dead and that He truly desires us to live with Him forever.

We do well to meditate on the wounds of Jesus so that we too can allow our wounds to be transformed by Him to be used for so much good. I love to reflect on the Mass of the Holy Five Wounds of Our Lord. This Mass was found in the Roman Missals approved before 1955. It was celebrated on the Friday after the third Sunday of Lent. Following are the prayers found in that beautiful Mass. I hope one day that the Masses of the Passion will once again be said by all priests

and bishops of the world to help heal our wounded generation!
Collect:

O God who, by the passion of thine only-begotten Son, and by the blood shed through his five most sacred wounds, hast raised up mankind, lost because of sin; grant, we beseech thee, that we who on earth adore the wounds of our Saviour received, may in heaven rejoice in the glory He, at the price of His precious blood, hath brought back for us.

Secret:

May our oblation, O Lord, find favor in the sight of Thy divine majesty; for we lay before thee the very price paid for our ransom, the five wounds of thine only-begotten Son.

Post-Communion:

Fed with bread from heaven, we beseech thee, O Lord our God, that we who to this day devoutly do honor to the sacred wounds of our Lord Jesus Christ, may henceforth, by the fervor of our life, show forth that we bear those same sacred wounds graven in our hearts.

Ad Jesum per Mariam,

Fr. Lawrence Carney

A NOTE FROM THE EDITOR FOR THE REVISED EDITION

We were frankly astonished at the warm reception and the huge amount of positive feedback with which the first edition of "Healing" was greeted. I was inspired to assemble that work by my own experiences: like so many others in these troubled times, I myself was extremely wounded, when by the grace of God, I first learned about, and then started on the healing journey preached by Fr. Wolfe.

Then – to my great surprise, bewilderment, and joy - a broken sinner like me suddenly experienced the love and peace of Christ; my heart and soul filled with a profound experience of being loved and cherished, of being loved for nothing more than just being who I am. At the same time, I found myself healed of so many of the wounds I had picked up in life, many of which, in my own ignorance, stupidity and sin, I had inflicted on myself. (Of course, my journey continued (and continues) with its ups and downs, with its consolations and desolations, with other wounds to heal, or some wounds which have healed to some degree still needing healing at a deeper level.)

Having been so deeply impacted (actually transformed) by Christ, having experienced the incredible healing charity of Christ, I felt compelled to share this as widely as possible.

Inspired by my own experience, I set out on this project almost 10 years ago, originally intending to transcribe all the healing sermons and conferences of Fr. Wolfe, in the hopes that they might help other wounded souls also experience that healing touch of Christ in their lives. Ultimately I chose to arrange the chapters topically, a decision we have also followed in this edition.

In this new edition, I have done some minor editing, added an appendix with some healing blessings useful for priests and deacons, moved a chapter that seemed out of place, added some important reflections and an important new chapter that I had somehow neglected to insert when assembling the first edition. In order to make this more user-friendly for those on the healing journey, I have placed a short explanation on how to use this work most effectively, and in the appendix, among other things, I have assembled a list of the healing prayers suggested throughout the work, as well as leaving a number of blank pages for personal notes.

Our sincere hope and prayer is that this revised edition will be an even more user-friendly guide to healing, and that it will help many others to make great progress on their healing journey.

A special note of thanks and gratitude to Fr. Carney for so graciously agreeing to write the foreword.

And as I stated in the first edition, any flaws or mistakes herein are mine.

Finally: there's no better time to start on the healing journey than right now.

In the Sacred and Immaculate Hearts,
the editor

A NOTE FROM THE EDITOR

(from the 1st Edition)

What follows is a series of short chapters, cobbled together ("cut, pasted, and edited" as he says so often) from the sermons and spiritual conferences of Fr. Phil Wolfe.

I had originally considered simply transcribing all his sermons and conferences that touched on healing, but after having assembled them, it seemed that there would be much too much repetition for a printed work, so I decided to assemble the chapters topically, taking excerpts – anything from snippets to almost complete sermons – from the various talks.

That decision involved a great deal of cutting and pasting. In his sermons, Father Wolfe often repeats points for emphasis, but for the most part, these have been edited out. I did my best to remain faithful to the message while adding some transitional paragraphs for the sake of clarity. There is still some repetition but it seemed unavoidable. I made no effort to locate the sources of his quotes; for the most part, they're given as preached. Any flaws or mistakes herein are mine.

In your charity, I would ask you to please say a 'Hail Mary' for Father. I am truly grateful to God and Our Lady for all that you will find in here, because what he's saying here, in this little work, really works. It's absolutely amazing: I speak from personal experience. If you really want to heal, if you really want to have a truly deep and profound relationship with Jesus, if you really want to climb Mount Carmel, just take all this to heart. Try it; you'll see.

And start today.

Other resources recommended by Fr. Wolfe:

Fr. Jacques Philippe:
Searching for and Maintaining Peace
Interior Freedom
The Way of Trust and Love
Real Mercy
Trusting God in the Present

Fr. Chad Ripperger: Talks on wounds and healing at https://sensustraditionis.org/release/wounds-and-healing/

Blessed Dom Columba Marmion. *Suffering with Christ*

Roberto Zanini. *Bakhita: From Slave to Saint*

Fr. Jean-Baptiste Saint-Jure & St. Claude La Colombiere. *Trustful Surrender to Divine Providence*

Pere Jean du Coeur de Jesus D'Elbee. *I Believe in Love*

Benedict Baur, OSB. Brotherly Love, found in *In Silence with God*

St. Alphonsus Liguori. *Uniformity with God's Will*

Fr. Jean Pierre de Caussade. *Abandonment to Divine Providence*

Sermons and talks on healing by Fr. Wolfe are available many places on line.

HOW TO USE THIS BOOK

If you want to derive the most benefit from this little work, please start by consecrating everything to Our Lady. This does not have to be anything complicated – a simple "Blessed Mother, I consecrate all this to you" will suffice. Feel free to use whatever title speaks to you most particularly: Our Lady of Sorrows, Our Lady of Guadalupe, Our Lady of Fatima, etc. Be sure to repeat that little consecration every time you pick up this book, and most importantly, any and every time you pray for healing. It's very important to entrust this work to Her.

Once you've done that, then read this book from the Introduction right through to the Closing Observations so you have a thorough overview – a sort of "road-map" - of the healing journey. Be sure to flip through the appendix to make yourself familiar with its contents.

After having familiarized yourself with the whole work, then begin your healing journey by entrusting it all to Our Lady, and then re-read this work, slowly and prayerfully, working your way through each chapter, jotting down notes and your observations in the back section of the book.

Note that on page 135 in the appendix you can find, in one place, examples of the various healing prayers scattered throughout the work.

Don't wait – start your journey today.

Introduction

Heal me, O Lord, and I shall be healed.
Jeremiah 17:14

We all want to be happy; we all want to be loved; we all want to be free.

All those desires are written in the very heart of man; they're our deepest and most profound aspirations.

But you don't need me to tell you that something is really wrong here. Really wrong. It's obvious from even the most casual glance at our society today.

Instead of happiness, we see so much existential misery, unhappiness, and lives of quiet desperation.

Instead of love, we see loneliness, abandonment, and emptiness.

Instead of freedom, we see bondage to vices and sin, and distress and turmoil over the exploding social chaos.

And the pain and emptiness visible in so many eyes, the unhappy faces, the agitation and bustling about, the broken marriages and shattered families, the perversions and hypersexualization of our society, the unreasonable anger and violence, the popular music and forms of entertainment, the drugs and drunkenness, the dark, ugly clothing, the tattoos and piercings, the empty wombs, the empty seminaries, the empty cloisters, the empty pews, are all just visible signs of the inner emptiness and unhappiness, of the living wreckage of so many lives meant for happiness, love, and freedom.

And every one of these people wants to be loved, every one of these people was created to be loved, but for the most part, they're not experiencing that, and they don't even know how to experience that.

Why all this chaos and sin going on every night, and most especially on weekends? Because everyone wants to be loved. They need that love; they were created for that love, but they don't know where to find it and so they're trying to fill that empty place, grasping at pleasures or deadening the pain and distracting themselves with loud music or drinking or drugs.

Everyone wants to be loved. Everyone needs to be loved. Everyone was created to be loved.

Let's bring that a little closer to home. How many of you are truly happy? How many of you have a deep inner peace? How many of you manage to keep your peace - no matter how troubling the affairs in the church, state or even your own homes? How many of you feel the Love of God? How many of you truly experience that Love?

We all want to be happy. We all want to be loved. We all want to be free.

All those desires are written in the very heart of man; they're our deepest and most profound aspirations and yet – at least in my pastoral experience – there are very, very few people who can truly say that they are happy, they are loved, they are free.

Why is this so rare?

In this little work, we've assembled a series of reflections to help us understand why so few have those experiences, and – more importantly – what each one of us can do about that, what each one of us can do to begin to actually experience that true happiness, that true love, that deep and lasting interior peace and freedom.

In his brilliant work *Interior Freedom*, Fr. Jacques Philippe – a man I consider to be the most penetrating spiritual writer living today – writes of the interior "space of freedom" that God has given to each one of us, and that irregardless of how unfavorable our exterior circumstances may be, if we learn how "to let this inner space of freedom unfold", we will truly be free, free to experience true happiness.

But the sad fact of the matter is very, very few of us have learned to let this inner space of freedom truly unfold, and this is actually why there are so few people who can truly say that they are happy, that they are loved, that they are free.

What we are saying, in other words, is that if someone does learn how to let this inner space of freedom unfold, then to the degree that this happens, to that very degree he will be truly free – to that very degree he will be truly loved – to that very degree he will be truly happy. And this in spite of the fact that at any particular point in time he may well be suffering.

So why – in so many people – is this inner space of freedom "folded up", so to speak?

In one word – woundedness. The reason why so many people have their inner space of freedom "folded up" - so to speak – is because of their woundedness.

In this little work, we're going to sketch out – in broad terms – a few ways for each one of us to approach the problem of our woundedness.

We'll only touch on some of the most important points, but we'll give everyone enough information to get a good start on the process of healing. After all, we all have this great desire to be healed, to be free of all the bondage that weighs us down, and leaves us sad, empty, angry, hurt, dissatisfied, and frustrated with people, places, things, even with God.

Healing and freedom await you.

Spiritual Wounds

But he was wounded for our iniquities, he was bruised for our sins: the chastisement of our peace was upon him, and by his bruises we are healed.
Isaiah 53:5

WOUNDS

Let's start with a brief discussion of wounds. There are two basic kinds of wounds: physical and spiritual. When you cut yourself with a knife, it makes a physical wound. The severity of the wound depends on how deep you cut yourself, and in fact, where you cut yourself, right? Over time, as the wound heals, the pain decreases until typically all that's left is a scar.

A spiritual wound is analogous to a physical wound. A spiritual wound is a result of a trauma or event in someone's life that left an impression that sometimes can be remembered, sometimes not... and the seriousness of the wound – the depth of the wound, so to speak – depends upon the seriousness of the trauma or the event. The traumas that cause such wounds can range from self-inflicted wounds resulting from sin (each and every sin wounds us) to wounds that have been inflicted upon us through no fault of our own – being violently assaulted, or even being conceived outside of marriage. (Yes, that does cause a wound.) But unlike the typical progression of a physical wound – from damage through healing to scar – typically a spiritual wound remains present.

Why is this?

Because – in spite of the fact that they cause pain – people usually don't know how to heal from spiritual wounds. But because a wound is a source of pain, we generally build barriers around the spiritual wound, so that we can live with, and protect ourselves from the pain. These barriers are typically expressed in certain forms of behavior or personality quirks which serve to protect us from that pain. To take a few examples, we might see them expressed as anger, resentment, fear or hatred of certain people or situations. Certain forms of dress, makeup, hairstyles, tattoos, or piercings are also exterior expressions of spiritual wounds.

So that's a very brief summary, just enough information to get the idea of what a spiritual wound is. For more details here, you can go to *Sensus Traditionis*, the website of Fr. Chad Ripperger, where he has 4 excellent spiritual conferences dealing with wounds and healing.

IDENTIFYING SPIRITUAL WOUNDS

In regards to woundedness, there is one more very important topic we have to briefly address: how to recognize the areas in our life that are wounded.

The question: "What are my wounds?" is a spiritual question. Some wounds are going to be obvious: if we were violently assaulted in childhood; if we had an abortion; if we grew up in a broken family; etc. But many wounds are not obvious. We need to turn to the Holy Spirit and Our Lady, and pray and beg, over and over:

Come Holy Spirit, help me to see myself as You see me, judge myself as You judge me, and love myself as You love me. Blessed Mother, help me to see myself as You see me – and love myself as You love me.

And over time, the less obvious problems will become apparent; in fact, oftentimes the person will become aware of previously unknown wounds.

This is really important, since there are so many different ways to be wounded, and many different types of wounds. Wounds can come from our families, and can be passed down, almost like an inheritance. For example, family pride. It's good to have a healthy pride/love for one's family – but a sort of arrogance can be ingrained into each member. Or a spirit of harshness, and so forth and so forth. Souls can easily be wounded by the loss of a parent, by being raised in a broken home, or in a home without love, or in a home full of violence in words and deeds, or by being abused physically, or emotionally.

Wounds can arise even *in utero* – in the womb. If the mother rejected the pregnancy, or seriously considered aborting the child, or even if she experienced a serious sickness or a traumatic sorrow, as amazing as this may sound, that baby can experience a rejection and may need healing from that. In both these cases, the inherited wound and the wound *in utero*, the family needs to be forgiven from the heart. We will have more to say on forgiveness in upcoming chapters.

There is a lot more that could be said, but this is sufficient to get everyone started on the right path.

The Most Important Thing

I am the Way and the Truth and the Life. John 14:6

In approaching the problem of healing from spiritual wounds, it's essential to keep in mind the most important thing, which is to recognize that the type of healing we are seeking is not some sort of New Age illusion based upon some sort of "contemplate your navel" series of practices – but rather an act of Our Lord and Savior Jesus Christ. We need to keep firmly in mind that we are begging for healing from Jesus Christ, that Christ is Lord, that He is a Crucified Lord, and that we will be following His bloody footsteps, which means, of course, that everything we do will be rooted firmly in the authentic spirituality of the One True Church.

In other words, we are presuming a serious approach to living as a practical Catholic: frequent confession (Padre Pio used to upbraid his regular penitents if they went more than 10 days between confessions!); fervent Communions followed by good thanksgivings; daily Rosary; good spiritual reading

(Lives of the Saints, Scripture, listening to good Catholic sermons and conferences); etc.

TRUTH

Our Lord is Truth Incarnate, and He will not bless or build upon anything but the truth, which means that since we are seeking His mercy and His blessings on our healing journey, we have to be open to the truth. It is simply impossible to heal spiritual wounds while remaining closed to the truth; we can't get anywhere unless we're open to the truth. So that's the first step in this healing journey: we have to make an act of the will to be open to the truth, no matter where that may lead. Depending on how rough a life we've lived, we may wisely suspect that we are not strong enough to embrace the truth about ourselves all in one glance – but we won't be asked to do that; we won't have to do that. We can take it one step at time, but we have to be committed to facing the truth, step by step, and eventually, over time, the whole truth. What is essential is that we remain open to the truth, no matter where it leads us. Again, it is absolutely impossible to make progress without this. And oftentimes, this is the reason people remain stuck in bondage, in their miserable, unhappy conditions. They just can't admit the truth to themselves. And until they do, there can be no real progress.

The kind of healing we're talking about is an act of God, but it requires the cooperation of man. And because God is Truth Himself, God will not – God can not – build on a lie.

So it is absolutely essential to be dedicated to the truth, no matter how painful or inconvenient it may be to us personally. Again, a lot of people bog down right here. They want things to be the way they want them to be – and not as they actually are.

AN IMMEDIATE CONSEQUENCE

One immediate consequence of the fact that spiritual healing requires us to be open to the truth, come what may, is that this will involve a certain degree of pain. Before you toss this book aside, please prayerfully consider what follows.

As we've just seen, because spiritual wounds are a source of pain, we typically build barriers around them so that we can protect ourselves from the pain and get on with life. That unhealed wound is lying there, behind the barrier we built. And when the wound begins to heal, those barriers are let down, bit by bit. And this process is frequently accompanied by pain.

It's going to hurt – but the pain we experience during healing is pain going out. When we were wounded, we were receiving pain; it was pain going in, so to speak. But as we heal, we are releasing that pain that we've been holding on to; in that sense, it's pain going out.

An image that might help to understand this is to picture standing on a cork, which is holding in all the bottled up pain and stress associated with the wound.

And as that wound begins to heal, it's as if the cork is coming out, and that pain begins to flow out. But keep in mind that this is pain being released

People will often call – and they'll say, in a worried tone: "There must be something wrong! Since I started praying for healing, I am having all kinds of inner turmoil."

But that's a good sign! This is a sign that the bottled up pain is being released. This is a sign of the re-ordering of that part of a person's soul; it's a sign of the pain going out, and Christ going in. And even though there may be stress and confusion at this stage, over time, the pain and turmoil will dissipate.

It's essential to keep drawing our focus back to Christ Our Lord, begging Our Lady to bring Him into our wounds to heal us. We'll take a look at one fruitful way to do just that over the next few chapters.

Forgiveness

Forgive us our trespasses as we forgive those who trespass against us.
cf. Matthew 6:12

One of the most important things in the process of spiritual healing is forgiveness. To heal, we must first be willing to forgive others – Our Lord explicitly taught us to pray: forgive us our trespasses as we forgive those who trespass against us. This forgiveness must come from the heart; it must come from the will. We don't have to forget what happened, but we do have to forgive and let that pain go.

That's important to remember: we don't have to forget what happened, but we do have to forgive and let that pain go.

Sometimes the hurt is too big, or too deep, or we don't actually know what's causing it, so we can't forgive or let go of it ourselves, and that is why it is so important on this journey to ask Our Lady and Our Lord to come into those areas, heal us, and help us to forgive and let go of the pain, to give it to them with an open heart, to will it with all of our being – truly will it! Desire it! In the spiritual life, the will is paramount. We have to will to be healed with all of our heart. Truly will it!

At times we have been hurt so deeply that we seem unable to forgive, but if we beg Our Lord to forgive for us, then our Lord will give us the graces over time, and those graces will enable us to be able to finally forgive.

AN ANECDOTE

Let me tell you a story to encourage you. Shortly after I was ordained, I had one of the most important conversations I have ever had in my life. I was talking to a priest who was at that time the only full-time exorcist in America, and he told me this story.

He was working with a young man who was possessed. And one of the things an exorcist can do (and no one else) is safely speak to devils (under the proper conditions and within the proper limits) and force them to truthfully answer necessary questions.

So, during the course of the exorcisms, he forced this devil to tell him what was required for the young man to be delivered. The devil laughed and said in a mocking tone, "He has to forgive his parents."

OK. But in his case, this was virtually impossible. Why? Because since his infancy, this young man had been subjected to torture, the most horrific torture: physical torture, emotional torture, other kinds of torture – unspeakable things – at the hands of his father and mother.

His parents were satanists.

And yet, in spite of these unspeakable wounds, within about a year of starting to reach out in prayer to Our Lord, that young man was delivered; in other words, he had totally forgiven his parents.

And I said to the priest, "Wow, Padre, humanly speaking, that's impossible! Humanly speaking, no one could do that."

And he told me, "You're right. But I taught him how to pray. I had him ask Our Lord, over and over again, to come into those wounds, to heal him, to forgive his parents for him and to help him to forgive them and to let go of all that pain. And over the course of time, Our Lord did just that."

And if Our Lord can heal someone that wounded, if Our Lord can give the grace to forgive those kind of abusers, then He can certainly give you the grace to forgive anyone who's wounded you; He can certainly heal you.

Let Him.

FORGIVENESS

As we forgive others and ask others to forgive us of any wrong, it is important that we try to repair the wrong we have done. If it's possible we should make restitution, not just because it's the lawful thing to do, but more importantly, when we right a wrong we are more easily able forgive ourselves and not have as much guilt to heal from. The effort to restore the wrong shows that we are truly sorry and want to be forgiven. It shows an act of the will. Humbling ourselves and asking forgiveness shows the same thing – if we ask with a contrite heart truly wanting forgiveness.

~

It is really, really important to recognize that with wounds of all sorts, especially the deep wounds, there is a need to forgive oneself, even if we did no wrong in causing the wound. This is essential to understand. It's not that we are guilty but there is a spirit of forgiveness needed where we can forgive ourselves and love ourselves in that hurt, realizing we can be loved in that wound. For example, if we were assaulted violently as a child we would have built barriers and personality quirks around that wound so we could get on with life and deal with the pain and trauma. As we start healing and we forgive the attacker, we will also have a need to forgive ourselves.

Now it might sound bizarre to say that in these kind of cases we have to forgive ourselves: Why would this be? How can this be?

As it turns out there is going to be a certain amount of guilt and shame associated with a wound – and in our brokenness, we actually blame ourselves for this. And we hold onto such a wound; we hold onto the pain, as if we deserve it in some sense – because it's our pain – it's our wound – and at some level we think: "No one else can really understand or feel the pain like I do, so it's mine – it will always be mine – and I have to deal with it all by myself; I have to do it alone. It's my pain and I have to bear it."

The point is that we need to be able to forgive ourselves, forgive everyone involved in the situation, and let the wound be healed.

~

It's also common, that if we've suffered a great trauma, we get the idea that we are dirty or that we have no value, and we may very well begin viewing ourselves like some animal or object. The results here are predictably catastrophic.

~

Or to take 2 other common examples, suppose a man was a real party animal in his youth, or a woman liked the effect she could produce by wearing provocative clothing (we're not talking ignorance here!) but later in life, they repented of their sinful behavior. It may quite difficult to be healed of this – why?

Because one of the typical results of these kinds of behaviors is a sort of perverse pride in that sinful way of life: a sort of perverse pride that he can drink and carry on with the best of them, or that she could really turn heads. And they may not want to let go of the prideful attitude, even though those sins hurt Our Lord and Our Lady. The point is that if they do not specifically want to let go of that pride – if they don't will it – they won't heal here, simply because this pride is associated with the wound. They actually can't heal here. And this may not be a fully conscious decision on their part. They must first have an awareness of what they are doing – and typically this will not come from themselves. A confessor, a priest, a director, or a good spiritual friend can point this out and help them to see it.

A very, very important step to understanding here would be to pray, inviting the Holy Spirit to come into their heart and life: "Come Holy Spirit, help me to see myself as You see me – and love myself as You love me." Then they must beg for the graces to completely reject this sort of prideful attitude – to be able to let go of it, and the perverse personality traits produced in response to it, these perverse traits that caused this person to take pride in disgraceful behavior and sin. They need to completely reject this because it hurts their relationship with God – it's a barrier between them and God.

~

Yet another common situation involves sins that after the fact, typically produce a heavy burden of shame. This is actually very common with certain types of sins: for example, cheating on a spouse, or looking at porn, or being involved in an abortion.

By way of example, let's consider abortion. Because of the shame, a woman who has had an abortion typically buries this sin deep within herself, but even in spite of that, she may often suffer anger, or depression, etc, from this sin. Although she may very well have confessed it, oftentimes she can not forgive herself. She believes God could forgive her, because He is God... but she can't forgive herself, and she is positive that others wouldn't forgive or accept her – if they were aware of what sort of things she had done in her past – and so she buries this wound deep within herself, hoping that it will never come out again. (Our country actually has millions and millions of women in this wounded condition; this wound is so common that there is even a term for it: post-abortal.)

The simple – and painful – fact is, that healing is impossible with a buried wound like this. She needs to invite Jesus and Our Lady into these areas, begging them to heal the sores, begging them to help her forgive herself and asking them to take this wound, to take all this pain away. She can even try picturing herself handing the whole situation, pain and all, over to Our Lord.

Surprisingly enough, it's actually pretty common in these situations for this severely wounded person to have a perverse sort of pride associated with such events. What do we mean by that? Well, the wounded person may very well think, in so many words: "I have hurt Jesus so very much that I can't burden Him with this awful wound and pain that I have created. It's mine – I did it – I caused it – and I deserve to have to carry this myself."

What has happened, in such a situation, is that the poor wounded person has become too proud to let Our Lord take her pain from her. In effect, she is saying: "It's my mess, and I am just going to have to take care of this myself. I pay my debts, so I can't really ask Our Lord to pay this for me, after all He has done for me. So I will deal with it, and then, after I get everything under control, then I can go to Jesus freely, without burdening Him with another debt."

Once we see this for what it really is, we can see that this is actually a terribly dangerous form of pride. To be fair, many times the thought process has not been worked out that clearly, but in any event, this is what she is doing.

She needs to clearly understand – she needs to clearly see – that if she were debt free, she would have no need for a Savior.

But we all have debts we can not pay – we are all in need of a Savior! We all have debts we can not pay, and Our Lord knows full well that we can never pay them. Besides, what on earth does He need from us? Nothing! He's God. He already has it all – He doesn't need anything.

So, in spite of the fact God needs nothing from us, in spite of the fact that God is perfectly content and happy in Himself, nevertheless, the Second Person of the Most Blessed Trinity, Our Lord and Savior Jesus Christ still chose to pay our debts.

~

One of the most important aspects of forgiveness is to not forget that we must be sure that we forgive God, from the bottom of our hearts.

Why would this be? How can this be?

This is certainly not because God has anything that He needs to be forgiven for – that would be blasphemous to suggest – but because oftentimes when we have been seriously hurt (as in the case of a child who has been violently assaulted) we blame God: "Why, if You love me, did You let this happen? You are God and You could have stopped it! Why didn't You protect me? I was too little to protect myself!" and so on and so on. This is very common.

In these sort of situations, we've placed a certain amount of blame upon God. And in our hearts, we are wounded and disappointed and hurt because God was not our "hero" in this case, and He "let" us get hurt. He let us down, so to speak.

Now this is certainly not the case – in fact, if we think about the Agony in the Garden, we can see that God was there in each one of those events, suffering with us, paying the price for the sin and hurting for us much deeper than we will ever know. (This sort of situation is roughly analogous to a mother seeing her child take a serious fall and get hurt – the mother feels the pain and suffering of her child – certainly in a different way than the child – but quite probably even more than her child feels it. It breaks the mother's heart that it happened.)

We have free will, which is an amazing gift. God doesn't want to take that away from us; He can fix our hurt if we run to Him, if we give it to Him fully, not holding anything back. He can and will fix it; He's God and He came to save sinners, to take sin away. The key is to let Him! Let Him!

We need to forgive God, so that we can trust Him and love Him. We need to be able to see that God didn't leave us, and that He is the only One that knows the hurt as we do. He understands what we went through, our pain, our guilt, our sorrow.

He loves us anyhow; He loves us in the wound. As a mother loves most tenderly when her child is hurt, so does Our Lord love most tenderly when we are hurt.

~

When we are able to forgive, we are able to let go of a huge weight that has held us prisoner. We are held in bondage by a lack of forgiveness, but when we truly are able to start praying and inviting Our Lord into these wounds, the barrier is slowly broken down and we are able to start forgiving and letting go of the pain. We are being set free.

~

One last aspect of forgiveness to touch on is the need to let others forgive us and to let God forgive us.

Sometimes we won't accept forgiveness. For whatever reason, we hold other peoples' faults over their heads and don't let them forget how they have wronged us. Such a grudge will actually prevent us from healing. When we don't let others forgive us, when we reject forgiveness, we are rejecting God in our life. It is even worse when we won't approach the confessional and let God heal us and forgive us. We think the sin is too big, or even worse, we don't want God's forgiveness. There is literally nothing that can be done here until we accept forgiveness.

~

There's much more that could be said about forgiveness, but that should give each one of us a pretty decent overview of the various challenges we may face here.

Living in the Present

Be not therefore anxious for tomorrow... Sufficient for the day is the evil thereof. Matthew 6:34

When we were kids, our dad worked as a packer and hunting guide, which means that he would take a string of pack horses and mules, along with hunters mounted horseback, back into the Montana wilderness. They'd set up camp with canvas wall tents way back in the mountains, probably about 35 miles or so from the nearest road, and then take the hunters out after elk and deer, maybe bear, whatever. Most of you have probably seen pictures of that sort of a thing.

One particular client made an impression on me that has never left. He was a great big guy, probably 6'5" and somewhere over 300 lbs. He was a retired colonel from the Army and at that time – over 50 years ago – that meant he had most likely been through World War II, Korea and maybe even a few years in Vietnam – and, if I remember right, he was some kind of war hero.

At any rate, at one point during his hunting trip, he'd shot a deer. So my dad took him up on a nearby ridge, and told him he would be back after he took care of the deer, gutting it out, getting it down to camp, and so forth. Dad showed him where the camp was and how to get back if he needed to, but in the meanwhile, he'd have a pretty good chance of getting an elk moving through there. They're both horseback. So dad tells him he'll be back later, and rides off to take care of the deer, leaving the colonel up there with a good horse, a high powered rifle, and directions to camp.

When my dad got back later that day, the colonel was literally terrified. He told my dad that even though he had been through war, he had never been so scared in his entire life: that here he was, 70 miles from the nearest road (actually it was more like 30 or 35 miles!) and that in his entire life he had never been alone like this before, that'd he'd always been around people since he was a little kid and never had experienced anything this terrifying in his whole entire life. It was so quiet. He had never been so scared in his entire life.

For the rest of the time he was in the woods, he wanted my dad right there with him, which, of course, my dad was happy to do.

He had a good horse, a high-powered rifle, directions to camp, and there was only a foot and half of snow or so. And yet he was plumb terrified, because it was so quiet.

This made a huge impression on me that's still with me some 50 years later. I could understand some of the fear, but the part that stuck with me was: Why would someone be so scared of the quiet?

What's so scary about the quiet?

I'm sure he's long since dead and I sure can't answer for him. But I can give a general answer.

A real quiet, a profound quiet like you can experience in the mountains – we don't call it the High Lonesome for nothing – a profound quiet like that can make someone have to face himself.

A profound quiet like that can make someone have to face himself: he can't turn up the music. There isn't any.

He can't turn on the television. There isn't one.

He can't head to the mall, or to the bar, or to the movie theater. There aren't any.

He can't distract himself by talking to anyone. There isn't anyone there. He's alone, alone with his thoughts.

And that can be a beautiful thing, but if someone doesn't have inner peace, if he's filled with turmoil over this and that, if and his usual means for distracting himself, his usual means for escaping having to think about his inner turmoil are not available, and all he has is that deep quiet and his own troubled thoughts, it can be very, very frightening.

And once someone understands that, it's easy to understand a lot of what we see in what passes for everyday life in our modern society. People filled with turmoil; people without inner peace, turning up the music, keeping busy doing this and that, moving around from here to there, playing around with all kinds of electronic gizmos – and all in an effort to distract themselves, to keep themselves from facing their interior turmoil and lack of peace.

LIVING IN THE PRESENT

Let's take a closer look at one common cause of inner turmoil. And, at first, it might surprise some folks: one common cause of inner turmoil is not living in the present.

In order to have true inner peace, in order to not be stirred up with all sorts of inner turmoil, we have to live in the present; we have to live in the moment God gives us – this present moment.

Now we're going to take some time to look at this in some detail, but before we do that, let's briefly consider why we have to live in the moment God gives us – this present moment – in order to have true inner peace.

Briefly then, if we don't live in this present moment, there are two choices: either, in some sense, we are living in the past, or in some sense, we are living in the future.

Now what does that mean, to say that someone is living in the past? By this, we mean someone that mentally looks back at his life and says things to himself like: "If only I would have done this", "Oh! I should have done that!", "Oh man I wish I would have never ever done that!", or "My life was so beautiful then" and so forth. In other words, when we say someone is living in the past, we mean someone who allows himself to be filled with regrets at his past failures or who wants to live in his previous glories.

So what does it mean when we say someone is living in the future? By this, we mean someone that mentally preoccupies himself by saying things to himself like: "What if this happens?", "Oh no, what if that happens?", "What will everyone think then?", "What will I do if he actually does that?"

In other words, when we say someone is living in the future, we mean that he allows himself to be filled with worries and stress over things which not only haven't even happened yet – they might never happen!

So the man who lives in the past allows himself to be filled with regrets at his past failures – or wants to live in his previous glories, and the man who lives in the future stresses out and worries about things which haven't even happened yet.

In either case, these men live in a sort of virtual reality: an "if only I had" attitude, in the case of the man living in the past; or a "what if" attitude, in the case of the man living in the future.

Although there are some differences in these attitudes (and we'll take a closer look at those shortly) either of these attitudes is absolutely guaranteed to produce inner turmoil: 100% guaranteed. Why? Because these past or future events are things over which we have no control!

These sort of attitudes hold us in bondage and prevent us from seeing ourselves clearly in the present, in the only moment in which we are living, in the here and now. The men who suffer from these attitudes are either trapped in the past, or in the future, but in any event, they are missing the here and now; they are living in bondage, in a sort of virtual reality. Either of these attitudes is 100% guaranteed to produce inner turmoil.

So that's a very brief overview of the problem. Someone like that doesn't have inner peace; he can't have inner peace, and so if he finds himself in a situation like the colonel in the quiet of the Montana wilderness, all alone with his troubled thoughts in a situation where he can't distract himself, it can really get frightening.

Now all this is actually a result of wounds. When we're hurt, we tend to live either with a regret of our past or sometimes with an anxiety about our future, and either of these approaches to life will leave us in a state of worry and make us unable to live in the present.

LIVING IN THE PAST

When a man lives with regret of his past, he in effect tries to give himself what he thinks he deserves, by not forgiving himself for his previous actions. The result is that he holds himself in bondage for his past, and won't let himself ever forget it. In this condition, he can't heal from those past actions, nor can he allow himself to live in the present, since at some level he is punishing himself, in effect saying to himself: "if I only would have done this", or "if only I had not done that", "I wouldn't be in this situation; I wouldn't have gotten hurt, so it's my fault." In effect, he has adopted an attitude that to be forgiven or freed would somehow mean that he would be off the hook for his mistakes, but in some sense, he doesn't believe that he deserves to be forgiven or freed for his mistakes.

So instead of trusting in the Mercy of God, and trusting that Our Lord paid the price and that He forgives us, in effect this man is saying: "Yes, Lord, You may forgive me, and You may have paid the price, but I got myself into this mess, it was a result of my stupidity, my decisions, so this is my hurt, my wound, my problem, so I have to deal with it."

But no one can change the past: it is what it is. And no one can "save" himself – that's why we need a Savior! By holding on to the past, by holding onto his regrets, the man is actually holding onto a wound and not trusting that Our Lord came to make all things new. He needs to face those regrets, accept that mistake, that catastrophe, that decision, that event for what it is, and then let go of it and let Our Lord and Our Lady take it.

How? By recalling the pain – not necessarily the details – but the pain, acknowledging it, and then allowing Our Lord and Our Lady to love him in this wound, in this event, in this decision. Obviously he doesn't ask Them to love a sin, but to love the wounded soul, to love that soul that is suffering from that specific hurt, to love him even in that specific wound and to ask Them to help him to let go of the past, to let go of that pain and turn it over to Them. And the wounded man needs to beg Our Lord and Our Lady for the grace to love himself – to love that wounded person that he has been shunning and that he has been so disappointed in; he needs to beg Them for the grace to see himself as God sees him and to love himself the way that God loves him – and most especially in that wounded area, in that hurt, in that regret that has been hanging over his life all this time, in those past mistakes that have held him in bondage. He needs to beg Our Lord and Our Lady for the grace to no longer reject himself, and to believe, truly believe that he is loved, even in this wound, even in this pain. And as this begins to happen, as this man starts to love himself here, he will be able to quit holding his past over his own head, he will be able to quit blaming himself for his troubled life; he will be able to quit saying "If only I had done this" or "If only I had not done that" and then start saying "I am loved. I am forgiven. Even with my past, I am able to grow in virtue and holiness right now. I am able to become a saint. My past is past. I am free. I can be holy. I am loved! I don't have regrets anymore. It is what it is, but it isn't controlling me anymore."

Let's not forget that the devil certainly promotes living in the past. Why? Because the man who lives in the past keeps himself in bondage; the man who lives in the past doesn't allow himself to grow in holiness, in other words, the man who lives in the past is actually unwittingly cooperating with the devil.

LIVING IN THE FUTURE

Now let's talk about living in the future. It's not uncommon for some people try to map out their future in a very meticulous way, worrying and fretting about every detail and possible outcome. Now it is true that we are supposed to take reasonable care for the future – but without worrying.

Because of the state of our society and the Church, many Catholics have lost their perspective and allowed themselves to become irrationally freaked out about the future, and their fears are fed by a great number of blogs, books, lectures, and even sermons. It is true that the priests are obliged to keep the faithful informed in the light of the Gospel, and this includes preaching on some frightening topics, like hell, or persecutions and even the End of the World. But even though these are definitely exciting topics, we're still not supposed to have a Chicken-Little "the sky is falling" kind of a tizzy fit when we think about them. That great Belgian Jesuit, St. John Berchmans, gave us a perfect example of how we're supposed to react when we think about these topics: one day, during the time assigned for recreation, as St. John Berchmans and his fellow Jesuit scholastics were shooting pool, one of them asked him, "Hey – if you found out that the world was just about to end right now, what would you do?" St. John answered, "I would keep right on playing billiards."

What's the point? St. John Berchmans was supposed to be taking recreation – and he was – and he was supposed to be in the state of grace – and he was. In other words, he was doing just what he was supposed to be doing at that moment, and the Lord expects us to be doing our duty when He comes again. So if we're in the state of grace and doing our duty, we're alright, and we should be at peace. But if we're living in the past, or living in the future, we won't have that sort of calm peaceful attitude, that trust in Divine Providence shown by St. John Berchmans. We'll be all stirred up and freaked out inside.

And yet, keep in mind that God knew exactly what He was doing when He had us live now. And He will give us every necessary grace to become saints in the historical conditions in which we find ourselves, if we will only ask for them and live accordingly. But instead, far, far too many Catholics allow themselves to be derailed by not living in the present moment, by not trusting the past to God's Mercy and the future to God's Providence – and instead they live in a sort of virtual reality – an "if only I had" attitude – in the case of those living in the past – or a "what if" attitude – in the case of those preoccupied and generally freaked out about the future.

So let's talk about living in the future. If a man is worrying and fretting and allowing himself to be dominated by all the "What ifs" - "What if this happens?", "What if that happens?" - this too is indicative of a wound. Because of his fears that things will not go right, that they won't go according to his careful planning, that they won't go according to his wishes, that they won't go according to his desires, that he will be wounded again, or that others won't accept or like him because things didn't go smoothly according to his plans, he won't be able to live in the present.

This is also a thought pattern which is very pleasing to hell. Why? Because such a man gets so caught up trying to insure that the future will be according to plan that he neglects to live in the present.

And yet this is absolutely essential to understand:

- The present, this very moment, is the only moment that we can grow in virtue.
- The present, this very moment, is the only moment that we can heal.
- The present, this very moment, is the only moment that we can gain an indulgence.
- The present, this very moment, is the only moment that we can become holy.
- The present, this very moment, is the only moment that we can become saints.

Sometimes I hear people say "If only I had lived here or there, during this time or that – if only I had known this saint or that! Then I would have, or could have, become a saint. If only... if only!"

When someone speaks like that, what he is actually saying – without fully realizing it – is that God doesn't know what He is doing.

But that's total blasphemy.

God knew from all eternity that we would be living now. And God sure knew exactly what He was doing when He had us live now. The present is the only time to become a saint! He doesn't change at all! His power hasn't been limited at all! As Scripture tells us, in Hebrews 13:8: *Jesus Christ, yesterday, and today; and the same for ever.*

Our Lord will give us every necessary grace to become saints in the historical conditions in which He has placed us, if we will only ask for them and live accordingly.

No matter when a man lives, he will be wounded. (Obviously we don't speak of Our Lady when we speak of being wounded.) No matter when a man lives, he will be wounded, and he will need a Savior, (and that does include Our Lady.) No matter when a man lives, he will be wounded, and he will need a Savior, and he will have a cross.

But the man who wants to be a saint has to make a choice. He has to stop rejecting himself and the graces of God. He has to stop living in the past with his "If only I had done this" or "If only I had not done that" - he has to stop saying "What if this happens" or "What if that happens" or "Someday it will happen" or "Someday I will work on my holiness." He has to choose to embrace his cross, and God's love and virtue, and invite Our Lord and Our Lady into his life to help him, to heal him, to guide him to sanctity. He has to choose to live in the present; he has to choose to live in this very moment, the only moment that he can grow in virtue. He has to choose to live in this very moment, the only moment that he can heal. He has to choose to live in this very moment, the only moment that he can gain an indulgence. He has to choose to live in this very moment, the only moment that he can become holy. He has to choose to live in this very moment, the only moment that he can become a saint.

He has to will it. He has to will it.

And he can only will that in the present moment, the only moment that we can become saints.

Attachments and Adjurations

For what shall it profit a man, if he gain the whole world, and suffer the loss of his soul? Mark 8:36

Another obstacle to healing arises from disordered affections. In this chapter, we will first consider exactly what a disordered affection is, and then we'll see how to break free from them. We'll rely on the teaching of that great Doctor of the Interior Life, St. John of the Cross.

ATTACHMENTS TO PERSONS

In his Counsels, St. John of the Cross notes that the world places several obstacles in the path of Union with God, including inordinate affection for any person, and disorderly affection for worldly goods.

God does want us to have affection for others, but in accordance with His Will. As Fr. Gabriel of St. Mary Magdalen explains:

There are some affections that are not only legitimate, but even holy and positively willed by

God. For example, the mutual love of Christian spouses, or the love of a mother for her children. Could it be the will of God that a mother not love her children, and that she forget them? No! If she should do this, she would offend God; she would commit a grave sin.

Blessed Lucas of St. Joseph explains the proper love of neighbor that we are all called to by Christ:

When selfishness motivates our love, it becomes narrow and limited and there is no room for love of others. When a man begins to love his neighbor primarily for the love of God, then his heart is liberated, and the capacity for loving embraces all men.

The more closely a soul approaches God by its sanctity of life, the more it resembles God. As God loves the entire human race collectively, and yet delights in each soul individually, so the true friends of God love all mankind, and also each individual. The saints excluded no one from their affections, yet they did not love each with the same degree of intensity. They had a special love for those who were nearest to God, but a paternal love for those who were most in need of it, because they were the farthest away from God. In proportion to their sanctity, three characteristics predominate: a sincere, practical love for all, a special love for those closest to God, and a paternal love for those in greatest need.

OK, given all that, it's easy to see that there is a distinct difference between legitimate affections and disordered attachments. A disordered attachment binds our heart to a someone in a way that is not according to the Will of God.

Suppose someone were to love his child in a possessive or a selfish way, or that someone were to make pleasure, and not love, the primary or final end of being with his spouse. These would obviously be disordered affections.

These sort of disorders can even be found in the most legitimate affections. One very common example of this becomes apparent when an otherwise good Catholic parent fights and resists a legitimate religious vocation of a child. Obviously, this would not be loving that child according to the Will of God.

ATTACHMENTS TO WORLDLY GOODS

These same principles apply to worldly goods, since God wants us to love all creatures in conformity to His will.

But in our troubled society, disordered affections abound. Countless people struggle with disordered attachments to food and drink, with disordered attachments to comforts and pleasures, with disordered attachments to such things as sports, other amusements, or social networking. Millions are so dominated by their disordered attachments that they have become addicts: to drugs, to alcohol, to porn.

Fr. Gabriel of St. Mary Magdalen points out that in general, God does not ask us to materially separate ourselves from things, (obviously one does have to materially separate himself from such things as pornography and illicit drugs) but rather He asks us to renounce every disordered attachment. The basic idea here is that we should own our possessions, and our possessions should not own us.

St. John of the Cross sums it all up:

> *The more a heart withdraws itself from earthly attachments, the more it prepares itself for the love of God and neighbor. When the affections are freed from natural motives, the soul loves creatures as God wills them to be loved. Such a love results in liberty of spirit and a greater love of God for His own sake. The deeper our love of God becomes, the more we love our neighbor, since the principle of both loves is the same.*

Real progress in healing requires a heart free from disordered attachments – a heart free to truly love God.

ADJURATIONS

Now let's apply all this to the process of healing. Besides healing prayers (which we'll address in the next chapter), placing our requests for healing in our rosary, and making frequent confessions and fervent Communions, formal renunciations are one of the most fruitful practices that we can use to speed up the process of healing. (The technical, 3-dollar name for this sort of renunciation is an adjuration.)

In this whole process of healing, we are learning how to allow God to come into wounded areas of our life. But since healing comes precisely from God coming into those wounded areas and healing them, another way of understanding healing is that it is a means of establishing a much deeper relationship with God in the life of a wounded person.

It follows, then, that we need to completely reject anything that hurts our relationship with God, anything that's a barrier between us and God, and one very powerful way to do that is by making formal renunciations.

Now before we explain how this is done, let's explain what we are trying to do when we make a formal renunciation. Typically, when someone is wounded, there is a disordered attachment (or series of attachments) that actually interferes with the healing process. So the whole point of a formal renunciation is to break free of that disordered attachment.

Let's consider an example. As we've seen, it is very common for someone who had been a real party animal in his youth to have a sort of perverse pride in his ability to drink and party. That perverse pride would be a disordered attachment, and would act as a barrier between that wounded man and God. So how would that former party animal go about making a formal renunciation of such a disordered attachment?

He would pray something along these lines:

I completely and utterly reject, with the full force of my will, everything that's disordered or displeasing to God in my thoughts, attitudes, and emotions concerning my rowdy behavior: I do this in the Holy Names of Jesus and Mary and in the Name of the Father and of the Son and of the Holy Spirit. Amen.

(He would repeat this 3 times: once in honor of the Father; once in honor of the Son; and once in honor of the Holy Spirit.)

He can use this same format with regards to other probable disordered detachments; for example, he could pray:

I completely and utterly reject, with the full force of my will, everything that's disordered or displeasing to God in my thoughts, attitudes, and emotions concerning my drinking.

(Or: in my thoughts, attitudes, and emotions concerning my promiscuity: etc, etc...)

I do this in the Holy Names of Jesus and Mary and in the Name of the Father and of the Son and of the Holy Spirit. Amen.

(And again, he would repeat this 3 times: once in honor of the Father; once in honor of the Son; and once in honor of the Holy Spirit.)

Now obviously he has to be serious here; he has to mean what he says, or this would most definitely be the sin of taking the Name of the Lord in vain.

Once the wounded person has "honed in" on the particular problem, the results are remarkable. What this accomplishes is the breaking away from the disordered attachment; the will releases, as it were, this disordered attachment. Oftentimes there will be a feeling or a sense of release or freedom when this is done, but this varies with individuals.

If someone has ingrained habits of thought, speech, or behavior that need to be dealt with, this sort of renunciation may have to be repeated several times a day over some time. And it should certainly be repeated after each fall, every outburst, disordered or sinful thought or act as a preparation for making an act of contrition. Establish habits of making acts of renunciation, followed by an act of contrition and prayers of healing after every slip, and fresh wounds will be healed rapidly.

And don't forget that disordered attachments are often present in even the most legitimate affections, which is why it is very useful to occasionally renounce anything disordered or displeasing to God in these areas as well. Certainly we do not want to renounce these legitimate affections, we're simply renouncing anything disordered that may be present therein. And we don't need to clearly recognize a disorder, we simply need to make the act of the will to renounce any that may be present. Some possible examples here would be to renounce anything disordered or displeasing to God in my thoughts and affections towards my spouse; or towards my country; or towards my favorite sporting events; or towards my love of food or drink; or my desires for my children's' success, etc, etc.

Establish habits of making acts of renunciation, followed by an act of contrition and prayers of healing after every slip, and in regards to anything you are truly passionate about.

And start today.

Prayers of Healing

And behold a woman who was troubled with an issue of blood twelve years, came behind him, and touched the hem of his garment. For she said within herself: If I shall touch only his garment, I shall be healed. But Jesus turning and seeing her, said: Be of good heart, daughter, thy faith hath made thee whole. And the woman was made whole from that hour.
Matthew 9:20-22

The healing of a wounded soul comes about by conformity and contact with Christ, by reaching out in prayer to Our Lady, and begging her to bring her Son into the situation.

We'll just quickly run through a very easy and fruitful method of doing just that. (It's important to realize that this is not a formula; it's only an outline, so you can adapt it as needed.)

Here's how it goes: we identify a wound. Let's say we were violently abused in childhood, and let's also assume that we have already worked our way through forgiving everyone involved. (Whether we speak of forgiveness or healing of the wound, it's the same basic process.) (It's also very important to realize that in the case of some sort of horrific trauma like this, we shouldn't try to call the circumstances to mind. That is not necessary and might even do more harm than good. We simply need to ask Our Lady to bring the Lord into this woundedness and pain and to heal us and make us free.)

We start by making an act of the will that we really want this wound and everything associated with it to be healed and that we are willing to suffer whatever it takes to be healed. As we've seen, we have to have it in our mind that this is going to hurt. Think of it like resetting a broken bone, but in this case, we're going to reset a broken bone in our heart, so to speak. Now we turn to Our Lady and pray: Blessed Mother of God, I completely open this wound of violent abuse to thee.

Then, we ask Our Lady: I beg thee to wash, cleanse and purify this wound with thy tears and the Precious Blood of thy Son

Then we ask Her: I beg thee to bring thy Son into this wound to heal it

And then we ask Her: I beg thee to fill this spot with charity, and together with thy Son to stay and rule.

It's really that simple.

Start today.

FORMAL PRAYERS OF HEALING

Here are two prayers that have borne real fruit in souls that I have worked with.

The first prayer came from an exorcist:

Lord Jesus, you came to heal our wounded and troubled hearts. I beg you to heal the torments that cause anxiety in my heart; I beg you, in a particular way, to heal all who are the cause of sin in my life. I beg you to come into my life and heal me of the psychological harms that struck me in my earthly years and from the injuries that they caused throughout my life.

Lord Jesus, you know my burdens. I lay them all on your Good Shepherd's Heart. I beseech you – by the merits of the great, open wound in your heart – to heal the small wounds that are in mine. Heal the pain of my memories, so that nothing that has happened to me will cause me to remain in pain and anguish, filled with anxiety.

Heal, O Lord, all those wounds that have been the cause of all the evil that is rooted in my life. I want to forgive all those who have offended me. Look to those inner sores that make me unable to forgive. You who came to forgive the afflicted of heart, please, heal my own heart.

Heal, my Lord Jesus, those intimate wounds that cause me physical illness. I offer you my heart. Accept it, Lord, purify it and give me the sentiments of your Divine Heart. Help me to be meek and humble. Amen.

~

The second is based on a prayer originally written by St. Clement Mary Hofbaur, CSSR:

O my Redeemer, the beginning and end of our faith, we beg of Thee, in the bitterness of our contrite and humbled hearts, not to suffer the fair light of faith to be extinguished in us, but turn Thine eyes in mercy upon the vineyard planted by Thine own right hand, watered by the sweat of the Apostles, by the precious blood of countless Martyrs, and by the sincere tears of so many penitents, and made fruitful by the prayers of so many Confessors and innocent virgins.

We beseech Thee, O God of justice, to hold back the decree of our rejection, and to turn away Thine eyes from our vices and regard instead the adorable Blood shed upon the Cross, which purchased our salvation and daily intercedes for us upon our altars. Dearest Mother, wash me in your Sorrowful tears and bring my Divine Savior into each one of my wounds, especially those wounds I am not aware of and those that have hurt me deeply, and with His Most Precious Blood cleanse and heal me.

O most merciful Jesus, relying on Thy promise that whatsoever is asked in Thy Name shall be granted, I ask in Thy Holy Name that Thou shouldst come into every area of my soul and heal me. Cast far from me anything that does not belong to Thee and help me to see myself as Thou seest me and love myself as Thou lovest me.

And in Thy mercy hear and answer me. Amen.

Today would be a great day to start praying these as well: just as the woman with the bloody issue was healed when she reached out in faith to touch the hem of Our Lord's garment, so also when we pray those prayers, we're reaching out in faith to Jesus, through Mary, and begging for a healing.

And if we're persistent, He won't refuse us.

A FEW RELATED POINTS

While someone is trying to heal from his wounds and seriously praying, asking Our Lady to bring Our Lord into each area and heal them, oftentimes previously unknown wounds will be revealed to the person.

Another point: if anyone has these kinds of wounds, and wants to discuss them with a priest, it is essential that – at least initially – it takes place in confession, under the seal. Keep it under the seal, so that not only is total privacy and security preserved, but also so that the Sacramental effects of the Most Precious Blood can pour over those wounds. Do not bring this out of the confessional. Keep it under the seal. It's safe and it's anonymous. Over time, if there is a need, the wounded soul might discuss the situation in the external forum – if – and only if – the priest is balanced and completely trustworthy; never start discussing these things with a priest outside the confessional. Do not risk getting wounded worse.

HOLY COMMUNION

Prayers of healing are especially powerful in preparation for, and in thanksgiving for Holy Communion. The Church actually makes the priest say a prayer for healing just before he gives himself Communion every time he says Mass in the Extraordinary Form: the 3rd prayer before Communion, called the *Perceptio* – contains the line: "Through Thy goodness may It (the Host) be unto me a safeguard and a healing remedy both of soul and body."

And everyone knows that beautiful line, which is found in both forms of the Mass: "Lord I am not worthy that Thou shouldst enter under my roof, but only say the word and my soul shall be healed!"

The 15 to 20 minutes that Our Lord is sacramentally present in you are priceless. Don't join the stampede to get out of Church. The donuts can wait. Spend those precious minutes praying and begging Our Lord to heal you.

Today is the day to start working on this. If you don't already have an intention for the next Mass you assist at, make it your complete healing. If you don't have an intention for your next Holy Communion, make it for your healing. Pick a major wound and start on it, today.

Don't wait; start today.

The Lord's Prayer

And it came to pass, that as he was praying in a certain place, when he ceased, one of his disciples said to him: Lord, teach us to pray... Luke 11:1

The best of all prayers is the Lord's prayer, taught to us by Jesus Himself. And Our Lord has placed a healing message in this prayer.

OUR FATHER

Jesus taught us how to pray, starting by reminding us that we are God's adopted children.

As we begin this prayer we're reminded that God loves us so much that He sent His only-begotten Son so that we could be healed and return to that loving relationship, that union with God that was lost by Adam, so that we could one day enter heaven.

He is truly a Father that loves his children and wants them to be happy. God is the Father of all fathers. He loves us and He wants a close, loving relationship with each one of us. His Mercy is greater than any sin we could have committed. He knows what we have done – and yet He still chose to adopt us and makes us heirs of heaven, as we read in Romans 8:15:

> *For you have not received the spirit of bondage again in fear; but you have received the spirit of adoption of sons, whereby we cry: Abba (Father).*

He, Who owes us nothing, loves us. We are reminded of this in John 3:16:

> *For God so loved the world, as to give his only begotten Son; that whosoever believeth in him, may not perish, but may have life everlasting.*

He wants us to know that we are never alone, that we belong to a big heavenly family who loves us, as we read in 1 John 3:1-2:

> *Behold what manner of charity the Father hath bestowed upon us, that we should be called, and should be the sons of God. Therefore the world knoweth not us, because it hath not known him. Dearly beloved, we are now the sons of God: and it hath not yet appeared what we shall be. We know, that, when he shall appear, we shall be like to him: because we shall see him as he is.*

God knows our hurts, our wounds, and our fears; He loves us and only wants us to be freed from these pains, free to love and to be loved, free to be the vessels of charity He created us to be. We truly are the beloved children of the Father.

WHO ART IN HEAVEN

We are reminded that we are the adopted children of our God in heaven, and we are supposed to fix our gaze on heaven. Our purpose on earth is to journey continually towards heaven, to strive for that union with Our Father in heaven. We should continually fix our gaze on heaven and never take our focus off that goal. As we move along our way on this journey, there will be many temptations to look elsewhere, to turn aside, to get all caught up in the things of this world, the things that pass away – and in the process lose sight of our heavenly goal. Losing sight of our heavenly goal is a very real danger: just pause for a moment and ask yourself how many people you know who actually keep focused on this destination?

We are on a healing journey to our Father's house in heaven, a journey to attain union with the Father, a journey to be set free in order to become the vessels of charity we were created to be. As we pray this, we should remember that we belong to our Father in heaven and that we are striving to enter His heavenly abode where He has prepared a room for us:

> *In my Father's house there are many mansions. If not, I would have told you: for I go to prepare a place for you. (John 14:2)*

HALLOWED BE THY NAME

We owe to God a debt, a debt of adoration, because He is our Lord and God, a debt of thanksgiving, because He is our first and greatest Benefactor, a debt of sorrow, because we have offended Him by our sins – and here Our Lord reminds us of how absolutely important it is for us to render unto God what we owe Him (by grace, and in our own completely insufficient way – we don't want to say something heretical here!)

The name of someone is more than just a word. A person's name represents and stands for everything that person is, and everything he stands for. A name truly stands for who that person is, which is why we should never hurt the good name of anyone – and it's also the reason that the Name of God is Holy.

His Name is Holy and should be glorified by us. We should not only glorify God by our words, but also by our actions and by the lives we lead. As the Haydock commentary notes:

> *The honor and glory of God should be the principal subject of our prayers and the ultimate end of our every action; every other thing must be subordinate to this.*

It is important for us on this healing journey to realize that we owe a debt to God, that God owes us nothing, and yet that He has made us in His image and likeness.

He has made us to be vessels of His charity, to love and to be loved. Jesus reminds us in this prayer that our Father is holy, that He is to be honored and loved by all men, and that He is a loving Father Who wants us to model ourselves after Him and to become holy ourselves.

THY KINGDOM COME

Our Lord is teaching us to plead for healing here. In this healing journey, we are begging for God's Kingdom to come while we are still on earth, and in that sense, we are praying that God Himself may reign in us, that God will reign even in our brokenness and wounds, that absolutely every aspect of our personality fall under His gentle rule and in so doing, experience His healing touch.

We are begging to be healed, to reach union with God. We can reach this union on earth, a union of love with God, described as St. John of the Cross as the "perfection of the spiritual life." St. John explains that

> *the more pure and clean the soul in the perfection of a living faith,* (*i.e.* the more healed), *the greater is the infusion of charity, and the greater the charity, the greater the illumination and the more abundant the graces.*

In other words, the more we heal, the more perfectly God's Kingdom will be established in our soul.

We should desire this and beg God to heal us, so that His Kingdom will come ever more perfectly into our life; we should beg God to truly reign everywhere in our heart and soul, so that we can attain that union of love with Him even in this life.

THY WILL BE DONE ON EARTH AS IT IS IN HEAVEN

Our Lord is teaching us that on this healing journey, we need to die to ourselves and we need to desire what God wills for us. Unless we do this, we will end up letting our little perverse personality traits and our wounds lead us around, in which case we will never be satisfied, we will never be truly peaceful, because we are not letting God be the King of our heart. When we truly want to be healed, then we want uniformity with God's Will and we can start healing from our hurts, wounds and perverse personality traits. We can finally become the person God created us to be; we can let "him" out (so to speak) to grow, free to love and to be loved. As we continue to heal, we will start living more and more for God. The Will of God will then come first in our life, and we will desire more and more to please God in all things. We will want, more and more, to give God glory and to render unto Him His due – not because we have to, but because we are being filled ever more with charity; we are being filled ever more with this desire to please God in all things because we truly love God as our Father in heaven. As we heal, we will open ourselves more and more to God, inviting God into every aspect of our life, and as the wounds are healed, God will fill those places with charity, until eventually we will be able to say with St. Paul, *"And I live, now not I; but Christ liveth in me." (Gal 2:20)*

GIVE US THIS DAY OUR DAILY BREAD

Our Lord teaches us to pray for what we need this day, in this present moment, in the now. And in this prayer, we are praying for all that we need to get through the day, both physically and spiritually. We are reminded that Jesus came to save us, that He came to heal us – if we but ask Him to.

And of course, this petition pertains in a particular way to eating. When we share in a meal with another, there is more going on than just eating together – more than just making sure we are nourished. A meal with another creates a real bond that is very significant; it's a special way of bonding that is unlike any other way to bond. We were made to bond in this intimate way, and even if people haven't given much thought to this, they still know it on some intuitive level, which is why people go out to eat together more than any other type of recreation.

Just think about it: what was the last thing Our Lord did with His friends before He went out to die?

He shared a meal with them.

And what was the last thing Our Lord did with His friends before He ascended into heaven?

He shared a meal with them.

Our Lord came to save us – and what better way to unite with us and let us know that He does not reject us, but accepts us completely, than to share a meal with us?

But even more than that, He actually gives Himself to us in an incredibly beautiful act of charity when we receive Him in the Most Blessed Sacrament of the Altar.

He actually gives Himself to nourish us and to come into every part of us, to fill us with His charity and to heal us. Make sure that when you receive Holy Communion, you invite Him into every area that is hurt and that needs to be healed, including areas you are not even aware of. And you should make a point of making spiritual communions throughout the day for this same purpose of inviting Our Lord in to heal you.

One easy way to to this is to ask your Guardian Angel to go every ten minutes to a holy Mass being offered up by a holy priest anywhere in the world, and to offer it up for your healing, and then return with a spiritual communion for that same purpose. You can easily do this every morning during your prayers.

Our Lord loves to be a part of our life, every moment of every day – not just Sundays and Holy days, but every day.

AND FORGIVE US OUR TRESPASSES

On the healing journey it is absolutely necessary to turn to God with true contrition and repentance and confess our sins and failings. Repentance is a necessary condition for the healing of those wounds.

But it's also essential to never lose hope, to keep in mind that no matter how horrible the sins we may have committed, Our Lord is still waiting for us with open arms, waiting to pour down His Mercy, His forgiveness, and His healing into our wounded hearts and souls, if we will but ask for it.

As Our Lord told the Spanish mystic Sister Josefa Menendez:

Sinners must never think that there is no remedy for them, nor that they have forfeited forever the love that once was theirs. No, poor souls, the God Who has shed all His Blood for you has no such feelings for you!

And that's true, no matter how many times we've fallen. Even if through weakness, we were to fall on our healing journey, Our Lord still waits for us with open arms; one day, Sister Josefa was lamenting the fact that she had fallen yet again,

Alas, I have fallen and displeased Thee. O Lord, wilt Thou forgive me once again? I am so wretched and can do no good!

And Our Lord responded to her:

Yes, my beloved, even your falls comfort me. Do not be discouraged, for this act of humility which your fall drew from you has consoled Me more that if you had not fallen. Take courage, go forth steadily, and let Me train you!

In one of her last letters, the great Doctor of the Love of God, St. Therese of Lisieux, tells a story which makes the same point. She says she wants to make a simple comparison to show how much Our Lord loves the imperfect souls who place their confidence in Him. She invites the reader to imagine a father coming to punish 2 disobedient, naughty little boys. The first runs away in fear, but the second boy, fully realizing that he deserves to be punished, runs to his father and throws himself in his arms, telling him that he loves him and that he is sorry for misbehaving and that he promises he will be good from now on. And then he asks his father to punish him - with a kiss!

St. Therese says she can't believe that the father could resist such an approach, and that even though he realizes quite clearly that his son will fall into the same faults, as long as the son takes his father "by the heart" so to speak, the father will always be ready to pardon him.

How great are the mercies of Our Lord! No matter how many times we may fall, let us never fear to get up, throw ourselves into His arms, and ask Him to "punish us with a kiss".

He is waiting with open arms.

AS WE FORGIVE THOSE WHO TRESPASS AGAINST US

As we've seen, one of the most important things in the process of spiritual healing is forgiveness. One must first be willing to forgive others. This forgiveness must come from the heart; it must come from the will. We dedicated an entire chapter to this already; in this part of our commentary on the Lord's Prayer, we'll consider forgiveness from the point of view of the love of our enemies. We don't necessarily have to be reconciled to our enemies – this could be dangerous in some circumstances, and even in the best of circumstances, reconciliation depends on the other party as well. It's also important to realize that although it is commonly said that we should "Forgive and forget", we certainly don't have to forget what happened, but we do have to forgive and let that pain go.

One of the first things we ought to consider is the very meaning of the words we are using when we pray this line in the Lord's Prayer. What are we asking for?

We are asking God to forgive us in the exact same manner as we forgive our enemies. Just consider what we would be asking God to do, if we were to refuse to forgive our enemies: "*Dear God, I won't forgive them for what they've done to me. So please don't forgive me for what I've done to You!*"

And in fact, Our Lord has even commanded us to love our enemies:

> *Love your enemies, do good to them that hate you: and pray for them that persecute and calumniate you. (Matt 5:44)*

So how do we practice this kind of forgiveness – this love of our enemies?

The first thing to keep in mind is that God never commands the impossible. He's commanding us to love our enemies. He didn't say anything about liking them. That's not the same thing at all: to love someone means to will the good for them; to like someone is simply an emotional response to that person. You can easily love someone without liking them. Parents still love their teenagers, even when they don't like them!

Do we love our enemies? Each one of us should ask himself: How do I react when I'm attacked, when I'm hated, when I'm mocked or persecuted, when people are making me suffer?

Am I consistently practicing the virtue of love of my enemies?

Or do I have a problem here?

As the late great Fr. Dion used to teach, (we'll follow him closely here) when someone's giving us grief, we should say this little prayer: "*God, make him happy in this life and the next.*" When someone's getting to us, we should pray: "*God, make him happy in this life and the next.*"

Remember, love is in the will, not in our feelings or emotions. We may still feel flaming mad at the guy who's tormenting us, but if we can say this little prayer, "*God, make him happy in this life and the next*", we've just done the most loving thing possible for that man, which is to pray for his happiness here and hereafter. Remember that to love someone is to will the good for him and by performing this little act we've willed the highest possible good for him, which is his eternal happiness!

Now someone might be thinking, "Oh but Father, I won't feel loving towards him."

Yeah, so what? Love is in the will – not in the feelings. As that great Bishop and Doctor of the Church, St. Francis de Sales, explains:

> *If I am told that someone has spoken ill of me, or that I am being opposed in some way, in an instant anger flames up, and every vein swells, but if amidst all this I turn to God, making an act of charity for the person who has offended me, there is no sin. I say, even if a thousand kinds of thoughts should rise up against this person, and not for the space of one day, but of several, provided that from time to time I*

disavow them, there is nothing wrong at all, for it is not in my power to check these feelings.

According to St. Francis de Sales, as long as we disavow these feelings, there is no sin. And so when we say this prayer: "*God, make him happy in this life and the next*", not only have we disavowed those feelings of anger or hatred or what-have-you, but we've grown in grace and we've grown in the virtue of love of our enemies.

Burn this into your mind: love is not in our feelings; it's in our will. When we say: "*God, make him happy in this life and the next*" – if we didn't will it, we couldn't say it!

There are 4 things that happen when we say that prayer. First, we grow in the virtue of love of our enemies. Second, by our prayer we've avoided committing a sin – perhaps of anger or hatred or what-have-you. Third, we are growing in grace by performing an act of charity. Fourth, we're obtaining graces for our persecutor, and we may never know in this life how much good such prayers will do for our enemies: when St. Stephen was being stoned, his prayers obtained the grace for Saul to convert, and become the Apostle St. Paul.

And of course we have the example of Our Lord to imitate: just consider how Our Lord treats us in the confessional. Isn't Our Lord always forgiving His enemies in the confessional? In fact, isn't that one of the major reasons He created the Sacrament of Confession – to save sinners, who are His enemies?

And think of what Our Lord said when He was being nailed to the cross: "*Forgive them Lord for they know not what they do.*"

Notice what He did not say: He did not say, "*Forgive them Lord, now that they've apologized and started being really nice to me,*" now did He?

And the same is true of the Lord's Prayer: it doesn't say "*forgive us our trespasses as we forgive those who trespass against us and then later apologize and start being really nice to us,*" now does it?

Notice what else it doesn't say: it doesn't say anything about forgetting. You have to forgive – but you don't need me to tell you that we won't forget; if nothing else, the devil will make sure of that. So you have to forgive – and if you've forgiven something, you will never bring it up again – even when you do remember. Otherwise you haven't really forgiven, have you? If you don't want God to be bringing up your old sins that He's forgiven, then don't be trotting out old faults of someone else that you should be forgiving. Use that prayer when you remember those problems: "*God make him happy in this life and the next.*" Don't be trotting out that old trash! (And if these sort of memories trouble you, make a point of praying for the grace to forget them.)

All you married folks, remember that when you took your wedding vows, you took a solemn oath before God and man to love each other for life. That's the same as saying you promised to forgive each other for life. And you don't need me to tell you that there will be plenty to forgive! The devil, the world and your own sinfulness will see to that. But don't be trotting out that old trash: get in the habit of praying that little prayer: "*God make him happy in this life and the next.*"

Remember: we are commanded by God to love our enemies. Love is in the will, not in the feelings. So when someone's tormenting us, or the memory of someone tormenting us comes rushing up – we can say this little prayer: "*God make him happy in this life and the next.*"

AND LEAD US NOT INTO TEMPTATION

As we travel along this healing journey, we have to keep in mind that we will encounter many obstacles that will try us, many obstacles that will tempt us to turn back. The world, the devil, and our own flesh will constantly be throwing up temptations to turn back. We have to keep begging Our Lord to lead us out of these temptations: we have to keep begging Our Lord to prompt us to call out to Him for His help in overcoming them; we have to keep begging Our Lord to give us the grace to never give up or to fall into despair.

We are asking for God's help to lead us out of sin and away from self, the devil, and the world, for God's help to die to self and let Him live in us, to lead us to His Kingdom, to lead us to heaven, to free us from sin, vices and perverse personality quirks that tend to hold us captive.

BUT DELIVER US FROM EVIL

Finally we are begging God to deliver us, to remove all evil from us, so that we can be free to love and to be loved. We are also praying that we be protected from evil, and although it may be all around us, and we may have to battle it, that we will be delivered from serious spiritual harm because we have been healed.

(On that note, since both our senses and our unhealed wounds are spiritual openings until we close them, a very good habit to develop is to make an act of the will to close yourself to any spirit that is not of the Holy Spirit, as a daily practice, and certainly when you go out in public or are exposed to the media. This will definitely reduce the effects of any attack.)

If we've invited Our Lord to live within us, and by His grace, we don't let ourselves be led into temptation, then we can have evil all around us and yet remain completely at peace within. As long as we don't turn our eyes away from the Lord, we can be sure He will remain within us, protecting us from evil and healing us through prayer and most especially the Sacrament of Penance (forgiveness) and the Most Blessed Sacrament of the Altar (our daily bread).

And we can be sure that if we want to be healed, and we keep asking Our Lord to heal us, then we will be healed.

AMEN

So be it.

Charity and Healing

And walk in love, as Christ also hath loved us. Ephesians 5:2

As we've said, the healing of a wounded soul comes from union with Christ: the question, then, is how can we attain that union?

St. Teresa of Avila explains that union with Christ comes by practicing charity:

> *The Lord asks only two things of us: love for His Majesty and love for our neighbor. It is for these two virtues we must strive, and if we attain them perfectly, we are doing His Will and so shall be united to Him.*

Love of God and love for our neighbor are actually two different aspects of the virtue of charity. If we are really serious about healing, we should be striving to constantly grow in charity, because the greater our charity, the greater our union with Christ, and the greater our union with Christ, the greater our healing.

Given the absolute importance of charity on the healing journey, let's make sure we have a decent understanding of what exactly it is, and how to grow in it.

CHARITY AND THE SUPERNATURAL LIFE

We've already seen that love is not a feeling, although feelings may accompany it; love is an act of the will, to will the good for someone. Charity (sometimes known as agape) is a very specific kind of love by which we love God and our neighbor.

What sets charity apart from other types of love? Charity is supernatural: God pours a strength completely and utterly above and beyond any natural powers into our will, precisely so that our will can rise above any lesser loves to the love of God and our neighbor.

The man with the virtue of charity loves God simply because He is all good and deserving of all love, and he loves his neighbor, not because he is fond of his neighbor, not because his neighbor is "lovable" in the common sense of that term – in fact, at the level of the emotions, he may even find his neighbor to be quite repulsive – but he loves his neighbor simply because God loves him. In other words, charity is a created share of God's own love for Himself and of His love for our neighbor, which enables us to truly fulfill Christ's command to "*love one another, as I have loved you.*" *(John 15:12)*

What does this have to do with healing?

Everything.

As we said above, the healing of a wounded soul comes from union with Our Lord: the greater our charity, the greater our union with Christ, and the greater that union, the greater our healing. So if we really want to heal, if we really want to be loved, if we really want to be set free, then we should strive to be so filled and guided by charity that it permeates every aspect of our life, until ultimately all our thoughts, words and deeds are guided by and flow from that virtue.

And it's important to remember that this is not natural, not in the slightest; it is purely a work of grace.

~

When we have the love of charity for someone, we love him as God loves him. We do not love him in order to be loved in return. So when someone truly understands charity, when he experiences charity in his life, he no longer fears "being rejected", because he is not loving another in order to gain love in return, but rather he is loving the other because that person is loved by God.

~

Let's take a quick look at a few ways to help us to grow in the love of God and of our neighbor.

LOVE OF GOD

Three practices that will help us grow in the love of God are detachment from the world, uniformity with God's Will, and mental prayer.

DETACHMENT FROM THE WORLD

A man whose heart is full of worldly affections thinks only of loving himself and satisfying his own desires, but the man who wants to have his heart filled with Divine love should remove from it all worldly desires: *For where thy treasure is, there is thy heart also. (Matt. 6:21)*

The simple fact is that to the degree our heart is filled with worldly desires instead of charity, to that degree our healing will be impeded. (Although we've already addressed this, it is so important it bears a brief revisit.) Detachment from the world means to bring our appetites and desires for created things into proper order.

Prayer is key here; pray to Our Lady, asking her intercession, and pray to the Holy Spirit begging Him to remove all desires for worldly riches, pleasures, honors, friendships, etc, from our heart and to replace those worldly desires with desires for Heavenly joys, holy friendships and spiritual riches and pleasures:

> *O God, before Whom every heart lies open, to Whom every will speaks, and from Whom no secret is hidden, purify, we beseech Thee, our hearts by the inpouring of the Holy Ghost, that we may come to love Thee perfectly and praise Thee worthily, through Christ our Lord. Amen.*
>
> (Prayer to Obtain the Grace of the Holy Spirit)

~

Grant, O Lord, that my heart may neither desire nor seek anything but what is necessary for the fulfillment of Thy Holy Will. May health or sickness, riches or poverty, honors or contempt, humiliations, leave my soul in that state of perfect detachment to which I desire to attain for Thy greater honor and Thy greater glory. Amen.

(St. Ignatius of Loyola)

Much more could be said here, but this is enough to get headed in the right direction.

UNIFORMITY WITH GOD'S WILL OR SELF-ABANDONMENT TO DIVINE PROVIDENCE

Growth in charity does not necessarily mean that we have to change a lot of our external behaviors and habits; what we have to change is the orientation of our heart, the focus of our will.

Naturally speaking, of course, every man tries to organize his life according to his own desires and his own view of how things "ought to be", but if we want to grow in charity, we have to re-orient our interior life, our goals, our desires, in such a way that we are always striving to live according to God's Will. This is easy to see – but not necessarily always easy to accomplish. Why? Because we're fallen: it's just not natural! This takes grace and prayer and perseverance.

St. Alphonsus explains that:

"Charity is the bond of perfection" (Col. 3:14); and perfect love of God means the complete union of our

will with God's: "The principal effect of love is so to unite the wills of those who love each other as to make them will the same things." (quoting St. Dionysius the Areopagite)

Love of God unites our will with God's Will. When our heart, when our will, has been definitively set to this orientation, then we can and will see that everything, whether good, bad, or indifferent, is actually a gift from God, and then we will be able to recognize that His plan is infinitely better than anything else, even if it may seem quite the opposite at times.

St. Bakhita's reaction to the incredibly traumatic events of her life provides a perfect illustration of this: in the middle 1870s, a happy little girl from Darfur, Sudan, was kidnapped by Arab slave traders. She was so traumatized by their violent treatment that she could not remember her own name, so they named her "Bakhita."

Over the years she was sold and resold, oftentimes enduring terrible beatings, torture, and even mutilation at the hands of her various masters; for example, one owner had 144 intricate designs sliced across her body, chest, and arms with a razor, and then for the next month, rubbed those bloody wounds with salt, leaving her with thick disfiguring scars.

After years of abuse, an Italian diplomat bought her, then gave her to another Italian family to use as a nanny. They took her to Italy, and while attending to business elsewhere, left her and the child in Venice with the Canossian sisters, where she learned that she had been created by a Lord of Love, a Lord that knew her and loved her. She learned that:

> *She was known and loved and she was awaited. What is more, this Master had Himself accepted the destiny of being flogged and now He was waiting for her "at the Father's right hand". Now she had "hope" – no longer simply the modest hope of finding masters who would be less cruel, but the great hope: "I am definitively loved and whatever happens to me – I am awaited by this Love. And so my life is good."*
> (*Spe Salvi*, by Pope Benedict XVI)

When her mistress returned to retrieve her slave and the child, Bakhita, now filled with hope, refused to return to the Sudan. The mistress tried to push the issue, but Bakhita fought, and in 1889, was set free by an Italian court. She was baptized and confirmed in 1890, and entered the Canossian Sisters, where she served as a sacristan and doorkeeper until her death in 1947.

A young student once asked Bakhita: "What would you do, if you were to meet your captors?" She instantly replied: "If I were to meet those who kidnapped me, and even those who tortured me, I would kneel and kiss their hands. For, if these things had not happened, I would not have been a Christian and a religious today."

Stop for a few moments and ponder her answer. Seriously: please don't keep reading. Set this down for a few moments and prayerfully consider that answer.

Is that not a perfect illustration of the truth that God is not thwarted by evil? When our will is in union with God's Will, then come what may, we can and will see that His plan is best, even if it might seem quite the opposite at times. Kidnapping and slavery actually led Bakhita to the Church, to religious life, and to sanctity: she was canonized in 2000; her feast day is February 8.

Obviously most of us haven't been abused and wounded in as dramatic fashion as St. Bakhita, (although in some cases, the abuse is certainly very significant.) And many of us are probably not able to honestly say that if we were to meet those who wounded us, that we would be grateful for what we've suffered at their hands. Many of us are just not there yet.

But we can be.

Pray for the grace to see every trial and tribulation as something God permits to help us deny ourselves, pick up our cross and follow Him. Pray to St. Bakhita for those graces, for the grace to conform ourselves to God's Will and to trust that everything that happens is for the good of our soul, the good of our neighbors' soul and for the greater honor and glory of God:

> *And we know that to them that love God all things work together unto good. (Romans 8:28)*

~

Before we leave this point, let's consider another situation, certainly less dramatic but more common than most people realize: a woman who had been in great pain for 30 years went to see Padre Pio. She told him that she was always in great pain and could barely get her work done, and asked him why she was so sick.

Padre Pio replied that every suffering is a favor, although most people don't see it that way. He explained that she had been suffering for the salvation of some of her family members: two of her brothers were leading terrible lives, the rest of her family wasn't much better, and her burden would be lifted in two more years, because by that time, she would have paid the price.

This is really worth meditating on: for decades this poor woman had been suffering with absolutely no idea that she had been making reparation for her wayward family members and obtaining for them the grace to have a holy death. God had sent her that suffering not just to purify her of her self-love, but also as part of His perfect plan to save members of her family that would have otherwise been lost.

Did the insight she gained from Padre Pio suddenly result in her being freed from the pain and suffering in her life?

Of course not, not in the slightest! But suddenly the spiritual beauty of the cross she had been bearing over the decades, and the deeper meaning of her life and all the pain she'd been suffering came into clear focus.

The truth is that God is constantly reaching out to us in every event, good, bad, or indifferent. If we truly want to love God in total abandonment to Divine Providence, then we need to pray for the grace to see and truly believe that each and every event happens because God allows it, that absolutely nothing escapes His attention. We have to surrender our will and pray for great faith, hope and charity, trusting that our loving Father will give us what we need, even if we don't understand; in the words of Padre Pio, we need to truly "*pray, trust, and don't worry.*"

That's easy enough to say, but what are we supposed to do if the cross is just pressing down too heavily? What are we supposed to do if the situation is just too painful to bear?

St. Claude de la Columbiere has an answer that might surprise you: in prayer, we should ask God to either take away our suffering, or to change it into a source of joy. He points out that the effect of such prayer is to give us a peace of soul and happiness in either event, and he asks: "*Can one ask for anything better?*" St. Claude insists that eventually we will receive this great grace, provided we keeping asking for it in prayer.

Suffering or not, weighted down by the cross or not, ask for the grace to truly love God in abandonment to Divine Providence. Pray for this grace insistently.

And start today.

Again, this is just enough to familiarize everyone with the basic concepts; for more information and deeper explanations, short but very helpful discussions can be found in *Uniformity with God's Will* by St. Alphonsus Liguori, and *Trustful Surrender to Divine Providence* by Fr. Saint-Jure and St. Claude de la Columbiere, while a very in-depth treatment can be found in *Abandonment to Divine Providence* by Fr. Jean Pierre de Caussade. These works are readily available, both online and in print.

MENTAL PRAYER

If we truly want to love someone, we have to spend time with him to get to know him; the more we come to love him, the more time we want to spend with him. In order to build and maintain our friendship with Christ, we have to spend time every day in conversation with Him. (Our Lord actually wants to spend time with each one of us: He loves us!)

St. Teresa of Avila points out that "*Mental prayer is nothing else than an intimate friendship, a frequent heart-to-heart conversation with Him by whom we know ourselves to be loved.*"

Daily meditation not only draws us into a closer union with Christ, it also helps us resist sin. Why? Because no one likes to hurt his friends.

There is much written on mental prayer to aid us in this practice; many have found *Conversation with Christ* by Fr. Peter-Thomas Rohrbach, O.C.D. a very valuable resource.

LOVE OF NEIGHBOR

On our healing journey, as we travel towards union with God, we also need to strive to see God in our neighbor. This is not always easy; as our self-love begins to be purified, it will be tried, especially by our neighbors: family, friends, co-workers, strangers or even enemies. (We've already considered practicing love for our enemies when we considered forgiving trespasses.)

A Passionist sister I know has some great advice for dealing with our more challenging neighbors: "*Sometimes people are a little 'thicker' so it takes longer to find God in them, but if you keep looking, you can eventually find Him!*"

In other words, some folks are more wounded, carrying more scars and pain, but no matter who they are, or where they've been, she makes a point of seeing the good in them, of "finding God" in them, and loving them there.

When dealing with one of these "thicker" people, we need to be particularly watchful over our thoughts, words, and deeds, to not get caught up in negativity and resentment towards him, but strive to see these situations as opportunities to bring love where there is no love, of finding the good in that person and loving him there. An interior disposition like this makes a huge difference in how we treat people and the words or actions flowing from such a disposition can really change the lives of those we encounter. The simple fact is that God wants to use us to pour some of His Love into the hearts of those we meet, if we just let Him.

So let Him.

When you encounter one of those people that seems "a little thicker", keep looking: eventually you'll find the good in that person, and then love him there!

~

Another important point: we should pray to always see every encounter with a neighbor as an opportunity to show God that we love Him: *Amen I say to you, as long as you did it to one of these my least brethren, you did it to me. (Matt 25:40)*

If our motives are truly to serve God in our neighbor, it actually doesn't matter how they respond to us. That may seem a bit strange; Mother Teresa explains:

> *People are often unreasonable and self-centered. Forgive them anyway. If you are kind, people may accuse you of ulterior motives. Be kind anyway. If you are honest, people may cheat you. Be honest anyway. If you find happiness, people may be jealous. Be happy anyway. The good you do today may be forgotten tomorrow. Do good anyway. Give the world the best you have and it may never be enough. Give your best anyway. For you see, in the end, it is between you and God. It was never between you and them anyway.*

In the end, it is between you and God.
Don't forget that.

OTHER CONSIDERATIONS

Don't be surprised if fears and temptations of various types arise when you're healing: "this is just too hard", "this will hurt too much", "it's too late for me", etc.

Don't let this discourage you! Keep in mind that as charity flows into wounds, fear is driven out. As St. John writes: *perfect charity casteth out fear. (1 John 4:18)* It may take time, but if you stick with it, as the healing progresses, the fears will get weaker and weaker until they disappear.

Keep reminding yourself that the only way to heal is to let yourself be loved in those wounds, with a heavenly love, the love of charity.

And keep praying – this too will pass.

~

Important points to take to prayer: pray often to grow in charity, for the grace to overcome your own self-love, self-interest, and to humble yourself, for the grace to see good in others, forgiving their faults and overlooking their failings, in a spirit of patience, long-suffering and forgiveness, for the grace to willingly give of yourself to help others in need, and to do all this with a smile.

~

As our healing progresses, we will be able to love ourselves ever more deeply in truth and charity, and to realize that we are indeed *beloved of God (1 Thess. 1:4)*, cherished by Him and more beautiful and precious in His eyes than we ever realized or ever could realize. As the prophet Jeremiah says, God has plans for our welfare, and plans to give us a future and hope. *(cf Jer. 29:11)*

We need to embrace the truth that we are loved, that we are really, truly, and wonderfully loved by a God Who knows us better than we know ourselves and Who loves us so much and desires so much for us to be healed and to come into union with Him that He came down from heaven to die for us on the Cross. It is essential to recognize that God does not love us for what we have done or what we might do, that He does not love us for what we have made ourselves out to be, but that we are loved simply for being who He created us to be.

~

Without love, we can not heal; it is absolutely impossible. It is essential for us to love and – what may seem strange at first glance – to allow others to love us in return. By far and away, the most difficult challenge for a wounded person is to let himself be loved in his wounds, and to actually love himself in those very wounds.

Here's a prayer we've already seen that can really help us overcome these obstacles:

Come Holy Spirit and shine Your light into my soul that I may be able to see myself as You see me, judge myself as You judge me, and love myself as You love me. Amen.

~

Why is it so hard for to love ourselves and to allow others to love us in return? Why is it such a challenge for a wounded person to let himself be loved in his wounds, and to actually love himself in those very wounds? We've touched on some of these points already in the previous chapters, but this is so important to understand, that it bears another look from a slightly different angle.

As we've seen, it is quite common to suffer from wounds that fill us with shame, a shame that prompts us to believe that we can never be truly loved for who we are. And most tragically, this also prevents us from accepting the healing and tender love of God in the very areas in which we need Him most.

But the belief that we can never be truly loved for who we are because of what we've done, or what's been done to us, is absolutely not how God sees things, as the Holy Spirit makes clear in St. Paul's 1st letter to the Corinthians:

Be not deceived: neither fornicators, nor idolaters, nor adulterers, nor the effeminate, nor sodomites, nor thieves, nor the covetous, nor drunkards, nor railers, nor extortioners, shall possess the kingdom of God. And such some of you were: but you are washed, but you are sanctified, but you are justified in the name of our Lord Jesus Christ, and in the spirit of our God. (1 Cor. 6:9-11)

Read that again, slowly; ponder the shameful sins in that list, and then think about what the Holy Spirit is telling the Corinthians – and by extension – us: some reading this may have been sexual profligates, some may have been trapped in the most shameful types of sins, some may have been drunkards or criminals or pagan idolaters, but whatever any one of us *might* have been, now we have been washed and sanctified and justified in the Holy Name of Jesus and in the Holy Spirit. (When someone has been justified – it's "*just as if I had*" never sinned!)

God sees us, He knows us and He loves us for who we truly are. Of course He knows us better than we know ourselves: He sees past all the woundedness and pain, He knows what we have been through and He truly loves us!

From the very beginning of the Church, God has been reaching into the broken and chaotic lives of sinners, washing, cleansing and lifting up their souls and their chins, and setting and guiding them on the right path.

From the very beginning. And He'll do it for you too.

Let Him.

~

God has great plans for each one of us: He longs to pour His life and love into our life and He longs to use us as His instruments to pour His life and His love into the lives of all those around us. The only possible obstacle that can prevent this beautiful plan of God from unfolding in our life is on our side: our refusal to submit to Him.

~

The whole goal of the healing journey is to surrender the woundedness we inherited from Adam, and the wounded life we made for ourselves, and in their place, to permit Jesus to live and love in and through us.

~

God created us to be vessels of charity. We were created to share in His love, to be united with Him. Each one of us has an innate desire to be filled with love, to love and to be loved, but since the fall of Adam, this desire is now disordered by our pride and self-love. We struggle to find a true, lasting love, a love that will satisfy the desires of our heart, a love that leaves a great peace and joy at the very core of our being, a peace and joy not of this world, but rather a peace and joy that remains even throughout the storms and trials of life.

The love of parents, friends and others can have elements of this charity, but all too often, these loves fall short. Unless and until we love others in complete union with God's love, there will always be a self-interested love that arises from our self-love.

~

One almost inexhaustible source of marital problems arises from a very common mistake: one or both of the parties look longingly towards their partner, expecting to receive a love and happiness that the other simply does not have to give. And the result is frustration and pain when that is not forthcoming. It is certainly not wrong or unreasonable to expect, to look for, to even long for that love and happiness – in fact our hearts were specifically made to accept and treasure those beautiful gifts – but ultimately these can only come from God. This love and happiness we thirst for can only come from God because it's actually His love, charity, that we desire. Only union with God, Who is charity can and will, fill our hearts' desire to love and be loved.

~

Our Lord Who first loved us freely, desires to be loved freely by us in return. Love has to be given freely: it cannot be forced. Unless love is given freely, it is not true love, so God has given us free will, precisely so we can freely love Him, Who loved us first! Each one of us has the choice of who or what we will love; God does not force us to love anyone or anything. God has first given Himself entirely to us, out of love for us. Christ has taken upon Himself all our sins and paid the price fully and all He asks in return is for us to simply love Him with our whole heart, mind and soul.

Each person decides for himself if he will let himself love and be loved by Christ. To be healed, to be free, to have true and everlasting peace and happiness, we have to let Christ live in us.

Let Him.

~

O Jesus, My Loving Saviour, You have so repeatedly said that You are thirsting for our souls, thirsting to continue loving, within us and through us, Your Heavenly Father, for whom You died on the Cross. You long to have millions of lives, millions of hearts to go on loving Him with, to the end of time.

I come then, O Jesus, to give and consecrate myself entirely to You, with all I have and am. May I henceforth be Your full property, not belonging any more to myself, but wholly to You, existing no more for my own enjoyment but for Yours. Do in me and through me all You wish to, and may I, fully identified with You, become like another humanity to You, enabling You still to love passionately Your Heavenly Father and Blessed Mother. May my eyes becoming Your eyes, look only at what You wish to see, may my lips utter only Your words – words of meekness, kindness and loving charity. May my mind be filled with Your divine thoughts and may my heart, dead to self-love, be aglow with Your ardent love for the Father and Your untiring zeal for souls.

Help me, O Divine Master, to do everything with You and for You. Make me obedient to Your Divine inspirations, so that I may at each moment fulfill perfectly Your least desires. Help me to forget myself and fill me to the brim with You, that, like the Apostle of the Gentiles, I may not live anymore but You alone live in me. In a word, be the life of my life and the soul of my soul. May my one desire here on earth be to express continually Your love to the Father, and my one joy to be Your joy, by giving You to God, to the Blessed Virgin Mary and to souls, through every act of mine. Amen

(Prayer from the book *One with Jesus* by Paul De Jaegher, S.J.)

Practical Examples

For I will restore health unto thee, and I will heal thee of thy wounds, saith the Lord. Jeremiah 30:17

Now with all that as background, let's make up an example of a wounded person, and then sort of walk through the process of her healing, of her "unfolding her inner space of freedom", so to speak. Obviously, besides the wounds of original sin, every one of us has a different "set" of wounds because of our different life experiences, but whatever wounds we may be dealing with, the process of healing is basically the same, so once we get an idea of how this works, of what sort of approach to take to woundedness, we can easily apply it to our own circumstances. There will be a significant amount of repetition of what we've already covered in the previous chapters, but it's all for the sake of illustrating the process.

So we'll imagine a woman named Judy, who at the age of 16, got raped and wound up pregnant. When her dad found out, he flipped out and demanded she abort the child. She caved in to his pressure and had the abortion, but complications set in, and as a result, she had to have a hysterectomy. She started drinking and became very promiscuous, but as the years roll on, she finds herself more and more unhappy; all her acting out begins to seem more and more gross and disgusting. She feels more and more empty, more and more used. She's miserable, just plain miserable.

Now obviously, before Judy's inner space of freedom can "unfold", she's got to heal – among other things – from the trauma of being raped, from the wound of her dad pressuring her to abort his grandchild, from the abortion itself, from the fact that with the hysterectomy, she can never have another child, from her disordered drinking and from her promiscuity. Judy is a very, very wounded person.

Is it even possible for someone as damaged as Judy to be healed?

Yes, absolutely. I've seen people heal from every one of the sort of wounds that Judy has. I've seen men and women heal who were even more wounded than Judy, some of whom have made it well into the heights of holiness. So yes, it is definitely possible for someone like Judy to be healed, and to experience a true freedom and happiness, to experience being truly loved.

~

So how would Judy set out on this healing journey?

As we've seen, the first step is the most important: Judy can't get anywhere unless she's open to the truth, no matter where that leads her. She may wisely suspect that she is not strong enough to embrace the truth about herself all in one glance – but she won't be asked to do that; she won't have to do that. She can take it one step at time, but she has to be committed to facing the truth. It is absolutely impossible to make progress without this.

Why?

Remember that the healing Judy is pursuing here is an act of God. What she's setting out to do, bit by bit, is to open herself to the Lord, to show God her brokenness, her woundedness, her pain and sorrow, and ask Him to embrace all of it, to heal it, and to take away that sorrow. In other words, she is setting out to willingly expose her wounds to God and to deliberately invite Him into the pain and chaos of those parts of her life.

Yes, it is true that Our Lord already knows what she's been through, and that He is waiting to lovingly embrace her in each and every one of those wounded places, but the simple fact is that He is so gentle that He won't go anywhere He hasn't been invited. She actually has to invite Him in, no matter how painful or inconvenient that may be to her personally. This doesn't mean she has to try to recall everything – this is not some sort of psychological exercise – but it does mean that over time, she will have to open everything in her life to Our Lord, and invite Him in, and beg Him to heal her brokenness, to heal her wounds, to take away her pain, and to fill those fractured parts of her life with His loving Presence.

Now with that in mind, let's consider 2 possibilities. First, let's suppose Judy's situation is much too horrific for her to face initially; and second, we'll suppose that although it is very painful, Judy can face her situation initially.

THE FIRST POSSIBILITY:

JUDY'S SITUATION IS JUST TOO MUCH FOR HER TO HANDLE INITIALLY.

Because of the damage and woundedness from the rape, compounded by her dad's rejection of her in her hour of greatest need, followed by the trauma of her abortion and the resulting sterilization, and her acting out, it's quite possible that of her own accord, Judy literally can't face the truth about herself: it really is too much for her to face; it really is too horrific.

She's wounded, she's traumatized, the person she looked to for love and protection and acceptance violently rejected her and conspired in the murder of his own grandson and ultimately the sterilization of his own daughter: it's just too painful. And, of course, at some level, she'll know that. That's probably the principle source of all her wild rebellious, sinful behavior.

She has to start somewhere. It seems like she'd be stuck, since she has to be dedicated to the truth about who she is, and that truth is way too much for her to handle. It's important to realize that in her situation, with this sort of horrific trauma, she shouldn't try to call the circumstances to mind; it's not necessary and might even do more harm than good.

What can Judy do if her life, her situation, is just too painful for her to actually face or even think much about?

We already considered this sort of situation when we considered the possessed young man from the family of satanists: she can use the same approach as that young man. Without trying to recall particulars, she should ask Our Lady to come behind the walls, into anywhere and everywhere that is wounded, praying along these lines:

I close myself to any spirit that is not of the Holy Spirit, and I beg you, Blessed Mother to please help me. I can't handle this, but you can. Please help me. I open myself completely to you and I beg you to come into my wounds and to cleanse them with your tears and the Precious Blood; I beg you to bring your Son into my wounds to heal me and to give me the strength I need to go forward and to be set free, because I can't handle this, but you can. Jesus and Mary, I beg You in Your Holy Names to please help me.

And over time, if Judy is faithful to this sort of prayer, Our Lady will bring her Son into Judy's life, into all her woundedness, and the result will be that she will heal and strengthen enough to be able to start facing the reality; she'll get the grace to persevere on this healing journey.

So that's the first possibility: the situation is much too horrific for her to face initially. And we're about to explain what her next steps would be, because this brings her to the starting point of the second possibility.

A COMMON PROBLEM

Before we turn to the second possibility, let's briefly consider a common problem for someone who is suffering from these kind of wounds; understandably enough, someone like Judy may have a serious aversion to men.

But Our Lord is a man.

So what should someone do who has real problems with men, who has a real problem (rooted in her woundedness) with inviting Our Lord into her wounds insofar as He is a man?

It's actually quite easy. She should visualize Our Lord as a child, as a baby. She should visualize Our Lady bringing in the little baby Jesus, or the child Jesus, into her wounds and woundedness.

(In terms of visualizing the Christ child during healing prayers, many women that I have worked with have found "the Bonnie Prince" to be a particularly endearing and encouraging image.)

THE SECOND POSSIBILITY:

ALTHOUGH IT IS VERY PAINFUL, JUDY CAN FACE THE SITUATION INITIALLY.

What should Judy do? She should pick a wound. Let's say the rape.

As we've seen, Judy needs to make up her mind that she really wants this to be healed and that she is willing to suffer whatever it takes to be free of this wound. Half measures won't do here; until she fixes her will on this point, she simply can't make any real progress, because as soon as things start to become painful and confusing, she is apt to give up and turn back. And again, if Judy is having a tough time fixing her will, she needs to beg for help using the same approach as above.

Judy needs to recognize that at certain points, the healing process is going to hurt, but this is because during the healing process, pain is being released and going out, whereas in wounding, the pain was going in. Her cross will be easier to bear if she keeps in mind that her pain can really be put to good use.

~

By way of encouragement, let's quickly consider one small anecdote: Yvonne Beauvais (later known as Mother Yvonne-Aimee of Jesus) was one of the most remarkable women of the last century; a mystic and a victim soul who – among other things – was given the mission to make reparation for those who committed sacrileges against the Most Blessed Sacrament. A 24-year-old woman waiting to be accepted into the convent, on August 10, 1925, she was ambushed and kidnapped by 3 men. They beat her, and tortured her, even to the point of pushing long knitting needles into her breasts. One of the men torturing her was actually a depraved priest whom she had previously tried to help by delivering him a warning from Our Lord.

He raped her.

She was tossed out blindfolded, on a deserted street in Paris. She'd been kidnapped, beaten, tortured, and raped by a priest, and tossed out on an empty street. She's waiting to enter religious life but now she doesn't know if she is pregnant or not. She doesn't know what will become of her, of her vocation, of her life.

In her journals, she wrote:

> *Jesus chose the heaviest cross, the most humiliating. I suffered atrociously in all parts of my body, in every fiber of my heart and my soul.*

But the most beautiful entry is her simple statement that:

> *After this trial, I obtained that same year the ransom of 32 souls of priests in danger.*

That pain didn't go to waste: she paid the price for the souls of 32 priests in danger – and priests have a very, very high price. As the old saying goes: Once a priest falls, he falls like satan, never to rise again.

What became of the reprobate priest that raped her?

Later, he repented, and was converted.

She paid the price for her rapist: a priest rapist. The pain didn't go to waste. The cross is easier to bear if you keep in mind that your pain can really be put to good use. When we're talking about healing serious wounds, it is going to hurt. But it's do-able, and it doesn't have to go to waste. And if you offer it up, it won't. And you could certainly pray to Mother Yvonne-Aimee of Jesus to help you here.

~

Let's turn back to Judy. Judy identified a wound; the rape, and she makes an act of the will that she really wants this to be healed. She knows it's going to hurt, but she is willing to suffer whatever it takes to be free of this wound. As we've seen, before Judy can get that deep healing that she so desires, she must first be willing to forgive everyone involved in the situation: her rapist, her father, the abortionist, and even herself. She doesn't have to forget what happened – she's not going to forget what happened – but she does have to forgive and let that pain go.

But it's very common for someone like Judy to be unable to let go and forgive. She just can't find it in her. How can she can finally "let go"?

By making formal renunciations. As we've seen, when someone is wounded, typically there is a disordered attachment of some type that actually interferes with the healing process, and a formal renunciation breaks the will free of that attachment.

Let's suppose now that she is working on forgiving her dad. She would pray something along these lines:

I completely and utterly reject, with the full force of my will, everything that's disordered or displeasing to God in my thoughts, attitudes, and emotions concerning my dad:

I do this in the Holy Names of Jesus and Mary and in the Name of the Father and of the Son and of the Holy Spirit. Amen.

(She would repeat this 3 times; once in honor of the Father; once in honor of the Son; and once in honor of the Holy Spirit.)

She can use this same format with regards to other probable disordered detachments; for example, she could pray:

I completely and utterly reject, with the full force of my will, everything that's disordered or displeasing to God in my thoughts, attitudes, and emotions concerning the rapist;

Or [in my thoughts, attitudes, and emotions concerning God;]

Or [in my thoughts, attitudes, and emotions concerning myself;]

Or [in my thoughts, attitudes, and emotions concerning the abortionist;]

Or [in my thoughts, attitudes, and emotions concerning the rape and everything associated with it and everything that flowed from it;] etc, etc.

I do this in the Holy Names of Jesus and Mary and in the Name of the Father and of the Son and of the Holy Spirit. Amen.

(And again, she would repeat this 3 times: once in honor of the Father, once in honor of the Son, and once in honor of the Holy Spirit.)

As we've seen, she has to be serious here, or this would most definitely be the sin of taking the Name of the Lord in vain in a very serious matter. What these prayers accomplish is the breaking away of the disordered attachment; by the Power of the Holy Names, the will releases, as it were, this disordered attachment.

(After going through the obvious problems, she should pray, asking her guardian angel, her patron saints, Our Lady and the Holy Spirit, to give her light as to what she needs to renounce, to give her light as to what her disordered attachments are.)

At this point, Judy is no longer "holding on" to serious obstacles to healing this wound, and it's time to turn to prayers of healing. She should Our Lady and pray along these lines:

Blessed Mother of God, I completely open to you this wound of rape, and everything associated with it, and everything that flowed from it.

Then, she asks Our Lady:

I beg you to wash, cleanse and purify this wound with your tears and the Precious Blood of your Son.

Then she asks Her:

I beg you to bring thy Son into this wound to heal it.

And then she asks Her:

I beg you to fill this spot with charity, and together with your Son to stay and rule.

This is especially powerful if Judy prays along these lines during Holy Mass and most particularly when she receives Holy Communion, and during her thanksgiving. The woman with the bloody issue was healed by simply reaching out in faith and grasping the tassel of Our Lord's garment, and healing power flowed into her; Judy is receiving the same Lord in Holy Communion – and He hasn't lost any power – He's the same yesterday, today and forever!

So if all it took was to grasp His clothing with faith for that healing power to flow out, is there any doubt that His healing power will flow out if we but reach out to Him in faith during the Holy Sacrifice of the Mass, and most particularly when receiving Him in a worthy Communion?

Judy needs but to ask, and she will receive. Yes, she may have to ask over and over again – but if she is persistent, healing will flow out from the Lord. She will be healed.

In that regard, it is important for Judy to recognize that she has to be persistent; she has to avoid a certain mindset which (in my experience) is actually quite common. Although this is slightly tongue-in-cheek, it goes something like this: Dear God, I would like to be healed, and to become holy. And I would like that to happen today (or by the end of this novena, or the end of this month, etc.)

I call this "drive-through" spirituality: "I'll take a healing and a holiness to go. I'm paying with this novena." And all too often, a person with this sort of mindset either gets frustrated and angry at God, because "He didn't come through" even after the novena – or they give up completely.

So Judy has to be persistent, and most especially when things start getting painful and confusing. If she's faithful, she will definitely start to heal. And as that progresses, the walls and barriers around the wounds start to come down, and pain starts to be released. This is a good sign; she's been holding it in all these years and now it's starting to sift back out. She needs to offer that up and keep praying, confident that over time, the pain will pass and in its place will be peace.

Over time, if Judy is faithful to these kind of prayers, day in and day out, this horrific wound will begin to heal, that "inner space of freedom" deep within her soul will begin to unfold. How will Judy know that she is healing?

She'll know. One of the easiest ways for her to tell is that she'll be able to think about the event, perhaps even discuss it with a close spiritual friend or her director, and there won't be any pain, any emotions associated with it anymore. Emotionally speaking, it will just be "something that happened", but the emotional bondage, the pain, the fear, the trauma will have dissipated. And that's a sign that the spiritual wound is turning into, or has turned into, a spiritual scar.

In this whole process of healing, Judy is learning to allow God to come into areas of her life that (because of the wounds) have barriers, so to speak, around them. But healing comes precisely from God coming into those wounded areas and healing them, so another way of looking at healing is that it is a means of establishing a much deeper relationship with God in the life of a wounded person.

SPIRITUAL COMPANIONSHIP ON THE HEALING JOURNEY

Another thing Judy should pray for is that God send her a good spiritual companion, a spiritual friend on the same journey, or a good spiritual director. She must pray for this; if she is truly serious, she will get what she needs... not necessarily what she wants. That's really important to realize at the outset, because when someone is starting on the healing journey, what she wants – what she thinks she needs – may indeed be nowhere close to meeting her actual needs, but in her woundedness she just can't see that yet.

Having a good spiritual companion, a friend on the same journey, or a good spiritual director is extremely helpful in the healing process, in aiding her to unfold that place of inner freedom in her heart. Judy needs to be able to accept and love herself, and part of that process is in being loved in truth, and accepted in truth, by another.

As Fr. Jacques Philippe points out: "accepting ourselves is much more difficult than it might seem." "We need to be looked upon by someone who says, as God did through the prophet Isaiah (43:4): 'You are precious in my eyes, and honored, and I love you'" and that "We urgently need the mediation of another's eyes to love ourselves and accept ourselves."

When Judy sees that she can be loved for who she truly is, and that this love is forever and will not leave her, this is a huge freedom. In that regard, let me tell you a little anecdote - and I do have explicit permission to speak about this. As it turned out, a priest got caught in a situation in which he had to hear someone's confession - face to face - while he was sitting at a table. Now unless the penitent is laying there in a hospital bed, that is just not something that this priest does. But he got caught in this situation, and the woman made a very good (and obviously painful) confession. And after it was done, since they were sitting at the table, they had something to eat together and just chatted and talked, joked around a bit. Some time later he ran into her and she told him that having that meal and that little visit after her confession was one of the most healing experiences, one of the most liberating experiences, that she had ever had in her life. And the bewildered priest asked her: "Why? All we did was eat and make a little small talk and laugh a little."

And she told him, in so many words, that it was so healing, because she had really come clean, really bared her soul to him, and so she was fully expecting to be rejected by that priest. She was convinced that after hearing "all that", in some way he would then push her away, but instead, he ate with her and joked around. And in that moment, she experienced a Divine Touch, she had an experience of the Love of the Heavenly Father; in that moment, she somehow realized that she could be loved for who she truly is – with a heavenly love, a love that will last forever.

How many wounded people have practically worn themselves out trying to not be rejected, and yet, in spite of their efforts, have always been let down? They've fallen into despair and sorrow thinking that they will never be loved and that they are unlovable, but suddenly – when they finally start experiencing that love of God for who they truly are – then they can start accepting themselves, forgiving and loving themselves and finally start feeling free.

INSIGHTS FROM SOMEONE CURRENTLY WORKING ON HIS WOUNDS

(When I mentioned to a priest friend, who has been following this regime of prayers, that I intended to assemble Fr. Wolfe's conferences into a little book, he generously volunteered to share some insights. *Editor*)

3 MANIFESTATIONS OF THE ORIGINAL WOUND

At the core of my particular wounds is fear. This fear is behind three "faces" of the wound. But first and foremost, the most vivid manifestation of the wounds is this overriding fear.

FAULT/GUILT

This first wound is based upon a difficulty with forgiveness, primarily of self, for bad decisions made in the past. Some of these decisions had consequences which were harmful to others, especially emotionally. Some of these decisions ended up being harmful to myself. There has been great degree of guilt associated with the past. The old adage, "Time heals all wounds" is not necessarily true. Even after bringing what needed to be brought to the sacrament of Penance, the guilt has lingered on. This is one of the devil's strongest weapons, and it is no accident that he is named, "the accuser." He throws the past in our faces, trying to manipulate us into a state of disbelief about the mercy and forgiveness of God.

WRATH AND REJECTION

The second wound deals with my childhood fear of my father's anger. First, a disclaimer. This is not a "blaming" rant. My father was a fine father in many many ways, and most importantly, he did the very best he could with the tools he had to be a father. Second, there was no physical abuse – no temper tantrums, tearing up furniture. But in the deepest core of my being, even from my earliest days of childhood, there developed a deep-seated fear of my father. Oftentimes, you couldn't really tell where you stood with him – is he angry about something? Is there something I have done wrong? Is there something I'm suppose to be doing that I'm not doing? I even remember going to my mother, when I was around 8, and asking her if dad really wanted me to be born. I know he did, and she reassured me of this. But one can see here the insecurity. This is why it is so critical for fathers to be active and positive in their kids' lives. He needs to be their guide and example, correcting when needed, but also showing fatherly guidance and pride in their children's achievements. It often seemed at times that my father's career was more important than his family. As I grew older, I saw that he was trying to do the best of his ability to be a good provider for us and he did a tremendous job. Providing for and taking care of his family were his priority, but I couldn't see it all in that light until later in life. In my younger years, and even into young adulthood, however, the wound that grew in me was that fear of not knowing where I stood with him. This at times led to real inner anguish.

My father was not the kind of man who showed anger often, but when he did, it was Hiroshima. He didn't even have to use physical punishment. The volume and tone of voice, when he was angry, was terrifying and went to your soul. And so, growing up, we knew not to get dad angry. Avoiding his wrath fed right into fear.

IDENTITY

This third wound is tied to the first two, and it is where the devil gets the most traction, and where he accuses the most. The first wound, that of fault and guilt, is where he exploits the mistakes/poor decisions/actions of the past. Dredging up these historical scenarios, he then uses them as a way to crush our identity. "You have played the part of evil so well, there is no good you can do now," "There is no way to salvage the wreck you have made of your life." Our true identity is based on our identifying with Christ, as He makes us a "new Creation." But the devil tries to eclipse this freedom in Christ with the past, even sins, which have been forgiven. On top of this, he labels us with labels that are not based on the Truth. All of this leads to a state of bewilderment and confusion of mind and soul.

What the Holy Spirit, and our Lady, can help us see however, is very important. All of the wounds that we bear in our souls have one primary source: Eden. We can trace back the wounds of our personal history to those of our first parents, Adam and Eve. What I have been given to see first and foremost, is that the fear in the core of my being is not my fault. It is the effect of the Fall I share in. Every member of the human race has in them a particular participatory wound inherited from Adam and Eve. Every one of us has some effect of the Fall which is in our spiritual DNA. These are all rooted in the sin of pride of our first parents which caused the Fall. This does not mean that we are not at fault for our sins – but it does mean that the spiritual darkness our souls often struggle through traces right back to the fall of Adam and Eve. In other words, all sin is rooted in the Fall. Some of us struggle with pride; others, envy. Some struggle with anger. And many people today struggle with fear and anxiety. And at their origin, at the root of sin in the history of man since God created him, these things are not our fault.

This is important to see, and I'm not talking here about personal sin or the free-willed decisions we make. Each one of us has some particular effect of the Fall in us. In my own case, recall the father issues. It is not infrequent that we hear that our image of God is often based upon our earthly fathers. In my own case, I had to deal with feelings of rejection by him (he really didn't want me/I've been nothing but a burden to him) and also fear of his wrath. Objectively, these things are not true. He did want me to be born, he was happy to provide for me in life, and he did the best that he could. And he, like all of us, had his own set of wounds to deal with. But it was given for me to see that the wrath/rejection theme of my father was also applied to God. This is connected to the first two wounds – Guilt/fault, fatherly wrath and rejection. Remember in the book of Genesis when Adam and Eve were kicked out of Eden. What would they have experienced? Guilt – their sin got them into this mess, and secondly, they felt the wrath and rejection of God ("Cursed is the ground because of you.") God was angry at them for their sin, and they were ejected from Eden. And at the moment of God's discovery of what they had done, their souls would have been filled with terror – a sensation they had never known before. The effect of original sin, living in me, is based upon these aspects of our first parents' actions – guilt/fault, wrath, rejection, and fear.

Where the healing begins, however, is to see the strange twist of this story. We have to recognize and understand that Adam and Eve are better off now than they would have been had they never sinned. Our first parents, who brought sin into this world, now have the Beatific vision, for all eternity. Recall that during the Easter Vigil Mass, we hear the phrase, "Oh Happy Fault." They walk with God again, with no fear, guilt, or shame. Their sin has put them in a better place than had they never fallen. This side of Heaven, we will never understand this fully. But for anyone reading this, with whatever wounds you bear, you must see that your glory in Heaven will be all the greater. If you have been a big sinner, and have turned back to the Father in this life, your forgiven sins will increase and magnify your glory in Heaven. Whether the wounds you bear are from yourself, or inflicted upon you by another, or both, even in this life you will bear even greater witness to the Father. By your seeking the healing of the Father, through Christ and His Mother, you will be an instrument of healing to others. It is critical to see this.

KNOW YOUR ENEMY

Ingrain this message into your brain, and keep it this simple: All negative thinking is from the devil. Write it down, put it into your Bible, missal, favorite prayer book, whatever. All negative thinking is from the devil. Evil is the absence of good. Therefore, any self-destructive, anxiety-ridden, fear-laden thoughts, any false self-identity labels, are from the enemy – the devil and his minions. Discouragement is one of his tools. One lesson I have learned through these processes of healing is the very real, destructive, wicked, and literally hell-bent wiles of the enemy. It is no accident he's a serpent – he hides in the weeds – moves slowly, trying to infiltrate the garden of your soul with ill-will, sin, and negativity. Don't be paranoid, but be vigilant. He goes about like a lion, seeking someone to devour. Resist him steadfast in your faith.

The healing process will not take place overnight. From what you have just read, I'm still laboring under all of the above. But the wounds have been identified. We prayerfully take them to our Lord and our Lady. Frankly, I'd like to be totally healed right now! But just knowing what the wounds are has given me a greater degree of freedom.

THOUGHTS OF ENCOURAGEMENT

If your wounds bear any resemblance to the ones here discussed, here are some things to reflect upon, which you can make into your own prayer.

Every moment of my life has been consecrated to Almighty God in order to give Him glory. All events – every aspect of my life, has pointed in one direction – to serve and love Him as His _____ (son, daughter, whatever your particular state of life). God has wanted nothing more than to shower me with His Fatherly love, care, and affection. To Him be the glory – Amen.

Finally, on a biographical note, I'd like to leave any readers with a message of hope. At one point in my life, as a young man, I had made some poor decisions which had painful consequences for others in my life. At a particular juncture, my mind was filled with bad philosophical ideas, and bad ways of looking at the world and dealing with others, even those closest to me. It reached a crescendo and led to some real trauma in my life. Much of this was based on my poor judgment. But my being was desperate for identity. Remember the wounds I talked about? I wasn't shown in my youth how to face the world – how to look at the world, and ultimately, what was the meaning of life - what are we here for. And so, at a point of desperation, I asked God to be my father. I wanted Him to adopt me, literally, as His own. I needed fatherhood. From that point onward, I tried to seek His will in following His Son, as best I could. It has not been easy, but I can say in all honesty that I have tried my best. I was ordained a Catholic priest some years ago. It didn't hit me until long after the fact, but I guess we could say that He did adopt me - forming me into an "Alter Christus." In His time, He has been showing me His Fatherhood. I will not know His Fatherhood perfectly in this life. And I still suffer from my wounds. But it's getting better - the healing continues - I'm a "work in progress." And for years, my earthly father and I have had a great relationship. We talk frequently, are very happy to be in each other's company, and I often ask him for advice - and I always get really good answers. That relationship has been healed for a long time. As I mentioned early on, please don't take what I have written as a "blaming rant" about him - again, he did the very best he could with the tools he had.

We live in very difficult and confusing times, and we need all the help we can get. But we have all been born into this time and this place to bring our wounds to God for the healing, to share our healing, and help one another along the way, until we all regroup in the kingdom.

Closing observations

This may not apply to every soul on this healing journey (although I suspect it does) but I just want to observe that in the experience of those wounded souls I have worked with that are faithful to these kind of prayers, at a certain point of time, there is suddenly a major (and for that person) a miraculous inner healing. They are lifted by divine grace, as it were, to a plateau; they're given a deep inner peace and a major healing: a major healing, but not a complete healing. The souls I am familiar with are given a deep healing, and a deep peace, but then there are still areas to work on, areas to which they still need to invite Our Lady to bring in the Lord's grace and light.

In my opinion, there are several reasons for this pattern of healing: in the first place, it's a great encouragement when that wounded soul receives this healing, when he really experiences that tender love of God, when he experiences that profound peace and love in the place of so much sorrow and pain; and in the second place, the fact that there is still "work" to do, so to speak, that there are still wounds left to heal also helps the wounded soul to see the necessity of remaining on that healing path, it helps him to see the necessity of continuing the journey, and it's a great encouragement to not fall into a sort of "Thanks, Lord, now it's time to get on with my life" mentality, to not to fall into that "drive-through spirituality" mentality of "I'll take a healing to go, and then I can finally get on with 'important things'."

The final point, a sad point: as we've already pointed out, we have to make an act of the will that we really want to be healed and that we are willing to suffer whatever it takes to be healed. I have worked with wounded souls that have made great progress, truly miraculous progress, that have been given a deep inner peace and a major healing, and yet – in spite of all the incredible graces and gifts showered down upon them – have chosen to turn back.

God has given us free will. He respects us and He won't take that away. He won't force us to be healed. He won't force us to forgive others. He won't force us to be saved.

He won't force us to spend eternity in heaven with Him.

Let's close.

Everyone wants to be loved, everyone needs to be loved, everyone was created to be loved.

In this little work, we've seen what each one of us can do about satisfying that desire, what each one of us can do to begin to actually experience that true happiness, that true love, that deep and lasting interior peace and freedom.

If someone like Judy can be healed, then so can you.

Life is short. Happiness, love and freedom await you.

Don't wait. Start on that healing journey today.

Start today.

Our Lord and Our Lady are waiting with open arms...

Appendix

A LETTER FROM A WOUNDED SOUL

Dear...

Praise be Jesus and Mary!

I am writing to you to share my experience with the image of the Little Bonnie Prince. He has been a very Big part of my own healing journey and I have personally witnessed how the image has brought healing into the life of a woman, who was badly abused in unspeakable ways by men in her life, from the time she was a little girl, from men she loved and trusted. This is a very hard-to-almost-impossible wound to heal from. And because of this wound, she just couldn't bring herself to be loved by our Lord. The thought of letting Jesus, as a man, into her heart was too painful and caused too much fear of being hurt; it brought painful memories of other men she loved and trusted and how they hurt her. Every time she tried, it brought up so much pain, that she just couldn't bear it, until I sent her an image of the Bonnie Prince. He melted down her fears and she was able to let the little Child Jesus into her heart to heal her from all those unspeakable wounds. She did not feel threatened by the Child Jesus and thru the image of the Bonnie Prince, she could begin a devotion to His Most Sacred Heart, (a devotion that was too painful before.) The innocent life of the Christ Child was allowed in, and embraced, and she did not have to fear getting hurt by a man again.

The image of the Bonnie Prince comes to the world at a very fitting time in history, a time when so many people, both male and female, are suffering from wounds from the lack of fatherhood, (both physical and spiritual fathers.) It pains people too much to let another "father" into their hearts, because all the other men have hurt them. The world is full of every kind of wound, but no one would fear getting another wound from the love of an innocent Child and they can turn to Him with open arms and allow the Bonnie Prince to bring charity into their wounded hearts that have grown cold, and in the process heal them.

I was pondering on how throughout history our Lord has come to us again and again reaching out to His people with such incredible love from His Most Sacred Heart. He came to St. Gertrude, St. Margaret Mary, and St. Faustina, all with the intention of bringing devotion to His Most Sacred Heart. Each of these times He has presented His Most Sacred Heart to His people in the way that was needed to renew devotion to His Sacred Heart. This time is no exception! The hearts of men are so wounded by the lack of love in their life and their hearts have grown cold. The innocence of our children has been snatched away like a thief in the night. The sheep are so wounded, broken and lost; they can't overcome the pain from the world (especially from men in their lives) and allow the Man-God into their hearts. But the little Child Jesus is not a threat to their already wounded hearts, so they can open their arms and let the Child embrace and heal them with His love – filling their hearts with flames of His love! The Little Bonnie Prince comes to the world – not as a threat – but as an innocent Child ready to help us bear our cross with love.

I have noticed how much the prayer blankets that I sew for others bring comfort to them; I offer the time spent sewing the blanket for the person I'm making it for and I sew a scapular, or religious medal, etc. into the blanket praying that they will be wrapped in love when they use the blanket. How much <u>more</u> comfort would people draw by clinging to the hem of the Little Bonnie Prince's tartan? Would be it possible to get permission from a bishop to bless the tartan of the Little Bonnie Prince so that wounded men and women could as it were, cling to the hem of His mantle, by wrapping themselves in His tartan and receive His healing blessing?

> *And behold a woman who was troubled with an issue of blood twelve years, came behind him, and touched the hem of his garment.* Matthew 9:20

> *And they besought him that they might touch but the hem of his garment. And as many as touched were made whole.* Matthew 14:36

Thank you for being the instrument in bringing the Little Bonnie Prince into the world and into my life. May His Most Sacred Heart be forever loved and praised.

In the Sorrowful Heart of Mary....

PS. I also found it very interesting that at least one priest wrote about using the image of the Little Bonnie Prince when working with wounded women and how many women that he worked with that had problems with men, could embrace the Little Bonnie Prince with love. (*Healing: Selections from the Sermons of Fr. Phil Wolfe*, p. 90.)

THE BLESSING OF TARTAN FOR HEALING IN HONOUR OF THE INFANT JESUS OF THE HIGHLANDS AND ISLANDS (*THE BONNIE PRINCE*)

This blessing may be given to any rectangle of tartan for personal use in connection with the Infant Jesus of the Highlands and Islands including a blanket, a shawl, a scarf and even a small piece of tartan that a person may carry about.

V. O Lord hear my prayer.
R. And let my cry come to thee.
V. The Lord be with thee.
R. And with thy spirit.
Let us pray.

Lord Jesus Christ, by Whose wounds we are healed; Who for love of **N.** (*or* us) suffered the internal pains of betrayal, shame, nakedness, mockery and to be spat upon; Who was slapped in the face, most violently wounded and abandoned to the death of the Cross; do Thou the Lamb who was slain, the Lord of lords and King of kings, under the invocation of Thy guise as *Infant Jesus of the Highlands and Islands,* our Prince in a plaid of many colours, deign to bless + this tartan of many coloured crosses, in token of Thy holy Resurrection and joyful victory over humiliations, sufferings and death; that through the radiant and glorious sign of Thy Cross, and through the invocation of Thy most powerful Name, Thou wouldst be pleased to bestow upon **N.** (*or* us), comfort, courage, the healing of (his, her *or* our) wounds, and an increase in (his, her *or* our) love of Thee. For there is no other name under heaven given to men, whereby we must be saved and through Whom victory is given. Who with the Father and the Holy Ghost, lives and reigns for ever and ever. Amen.

(With the permission of the Right Reverend Dom Hugh Gilbert, O.S.B., Bishop of Aberdeen, 4 May, 2020)

Appendix

BLESSING OF A SICK ADULT FROM THE ROMAN RITUAL

BENEDICTIO ADULTI AEGROTANTIS

Sacerdos cubiculum aegrotantis ingrediens dicat:
V. Pax huic domui.
R. Et omnibus habitantibus in ea.

Et continuo ad infirmum accedens subiungat:
V. Adiutorium nostrum in nomine Domini.
R. Qui fecit caelum et terram.
V. Domine, exaudi orationem meam.
R. Et clamor meus ad te veniat.
V. Dominus vobiscum.
R. Et cum spiritu tuo.

Sacerdos uti potest una vel pluribus ex sequentibus orationibus.

Orémus. Introeat, Domine Iesu Christe, domum hanc ad nostrae humilitatis ingressum pax et misericordia tua; effugiat ex hoc loco omnis nequitia daemonum, adsint Angeli pacis, domumque hanc deserat omnis maligna discordia. Magnifica, Domine, super nos nomen sanctum tuum: et benedic nostrae conversationi: Qui sanctus et pius es, et permanes cum Patre et Spiritu Sancto in saecula saeculorum.
R. Amen.

Orémus. Respice, famulum tuum, (famulam tuam) N., in infirmitate corporis laborantem, et animam refove quam creasti: ut castigationibus emendatus (emendata), continuo se sentiat tua miseratione salvatum (salvatam.)
Per Christum Dominum nostrum.
R. Amen.

BLESSING OF A SICK ADULT

The priest enters the room of the sick person and says:
V. Peace to this house.
R. And to all who dwell herein.

He goes directly to the sick person and says:
V. Our help is in the Name of the Lord.
R. Who made heaven and earth.
V. O Lord, hear my prayer.
R. And let my cry come unto Thee.
V. The Lord be with you.
R. And with thy spirit.

The singular or the plural may be used in these prayers.
Let us pray. As I enter here with a sense of my own unworthiness, O Lord Jesus Christ, may Thy peace and Thy mercy enter with me. Let the demons with all their wickedness flee from this place; let the Angels of peace be present, and let all hateful dissension take leave of this house. O Lord, show forth in us the greatness of Thy Holy Name, and bless whatever we do. Thou Who art holy and loving, Who live with the Father and the Holy Spirit for ever and ever.
R. Amen.

Let us pray. O Lord, look upon your servant, N., laboring under bodily weakness, and cherish and revive the soul which Thou hast created, so that, purified by his (her) sufferings, he (she) may soon find himself (herself) healed by your mercy.
Through Christ our Lord.
R. Amen.

Oremus. Misericors, Domine, fidelium consolator, quaesumus immensam pietatem tuam, ut ad introitum humilitatis nostrae hunc famulum tuum, (hanc famulam tuam) N., super lectum doloris sui iacentem, visitare digneris, sicut socrum Simonis visitasti: propitius adesto ei, Domine, quatenus pristina sanitate recepta, gratiarum tibi in Ecclesia tua referat actiones: Qui vivis et regnas Deus in saecula saeculorum.
R. Amen.

Deinde, extendens dexteram versus aegrotum, dicat:

Dominus Iesus Christus apud te sit, ut te defendat: intra te sit, ut te conservet: ante te sit, ut te ducat: post te sit, ut te custodiat: super te sit, ut te benedicat: Qui cum Patre et Spiritu Sancto vivit et regnat in saecula saeculorum.
R. Amen.

Benedictio Dei omnipoténtis, Patris, et Filii, + et Spiritus Sancti, descendat super te, et maneat semper.
R. Amen.

Demum aspergat infirmum aqua benedicta.

Let us pray. O Lord, merciful Consoler of Thy faithful, we ask of Thee in Thy boundless love that as I, Thy lowly servant, enter here, Thou mayest visit this Thy servant, N., lying on his (her) bed of pain, as Thou didst visit the mother of Peter's wife. In Thy kindness be with him (her), O Lord, so that he (she) may regain his(her) former strength, and be able to give thanks to Thee in Thy Church.
Who live and reign, God, forever and ever.
R. Amen.

Then, extending his right hand toward the sick person, the priest says:

May the Lord Jesus Christ be with you that He may defend you; within you that He may sustain you; before you that He may lead you; behind you that He may protect you; above you that He may bless you: He who lives and reigns with the Father and the Holy Spirit for ever and ever.
R. Amen.

May the blessing of almighty God, the Father and the Son + and the Holy Spirit, descend upon you and remain forever.
R. Amen.

Finally he sprinkles the sick person with holy water.

HEALING THROUGH DEVOTION TO THE HOLY WOUNDS OF OUR LORD

(*From "Sister Mary Martha Chambon and the Holy Wounds of Our Lord Jesus Christ"; Academy of the Visitation, Saint Louis, MO; 1924. Imprimatur: October 13, 1924, by + John J. Glennon, Archbishop of St. Louis.*)

These devotions and promises were revealed by Our Lord to Sr. Mary Martha Chambon, (1841-1907), of the Monastery of the Visitation of Chambery, in France.

Promises of Our Lord:

My Wounds will repair yours... My Wounds will cover all your faults... Those who honor them will have a true knowledge of Jesus Christ.

When you have some trouble, something to suffer – quickly place it in My Wounds and the pain will be alleviated.

I will grant all that is asked of Me through the invocation of My holy Wounds... You will obtain all because it is through the merit of My Blood, which is of infinite price.

When you have some trouble, something to suffer — quickly place it in My Wounds and the pain will be alleviated.

Rosary of the Holy Wounds

On the Crucifix and on the first three beads are said the following beautiful prayers:

On the Crucifix:
"O Jesus, divine Redeemer, be merciful to us and to the whole world. – Amen."

On the first three beads:
"Holy God, Holy Mighty God, Holy Immortal God, have mercy on us and on the whole world. - Amen."

"Grace and mercy, oh, my Jesus, during present dangers; cover us with Thy Precious Blood. - Amen."

"Eternal Father, grant us mercy through the Precious Blood of Jesus Christ, Thy only Son; grant us mercy, we beseech Thee. - Amen, Amen, Amen."

The invocations revealed by Our Lord are said on the other beads:

On the large beads:
V. Eternal Father, I offer Thee the Holy Wounds of our Lord Jesus Christ,
R. to heal the wounds of our souls (*my soul*).

On the small beads:
V. My Jesus, Pardon and Mercy,
R. through the Merits of Thy Holy Wounds.

ADDRESSING SEMINARIANS FROM THE PULPIT

Remember them, O Lord my God, that defile the priesthood... II Esdras 13:29

In this great cultural war in which we find ourselves, we have lost absolutely every battle.

Every battle.

In fact, with very few exceptions, we haven't really even put up a fight; we just surrendered.

Our culture is rotten, rotten to the core. It's not just bad, it's not just wicked, it's positively satanic: the collapse of families, divorce, contraception, sterilization, disastrously low birth rates, impure behavior from grade school to the grave, perversions galore, serial polygamy, perverted so-called marriages, perverted schools, legal fights over who gets to use a bathroom, black masses held in public places under police protection, federally protected altars of satan in every abortion mill, filth pouring out of the internet into homes, families, and lives, an immoral and even amoral ruling class, political candidates that could make a character in a soap opera seem normal and moral, economic chaos, immoral wars, violent and impure entertainment.

It all seems broken right now, and it's only going to get worse.

We've lost every battle, and for the most part, we didn't even put up a fight. We just surrendered.

Our culture is rotten to the core. It's not just bad, it's not just wicked, it's positively satanic.

It's reminiscent of the situation which prevailed in the time of the Prophet Hosea:

> *Hear the word of the Lord, ye children of Israel, for the Lord shall enter into judgment with the inhabitants of the land: for there is no truth, and there is no mercy, and there is no knowledge of God in the land. Cursing, and lying, and killing, and theft, and adultery have overflowed, and blood hath touched blood. Therefore shall the land mourn, and every one that dwelleth in it shall languish with the beasts of the field, and with the fowls of the air: yea, the fishes of the sea also shall be taken away... My people are destroyed for lack of knowledge: because thou hast rejected knowledge, I will also reject thee, that thou shalt be no priest to me: seeing thou hast forgotten the law of thy God, I also will forget thy children... And it shall be, like people, like priest; and I will punish them for their ways, and will requite them for their doings.*

There is no truth, and there is no mercy, and there is no knowledge of God in the land; there is cursing, lying, killing, theft, adultery, and bloodshed. Sounds just like current events, doesn't it?

There are even environmental problems: the land mourns, as do the beasts of the field, and the birds of the air, and even the fish of the sea perish.

And what caused all this? The priests. My people are destroyed for lack of knowledge. And since you have forgotten the law of your God, I also will forget your children. And it shall be like people, like priest; I will punish them for their ways, and repay them for their doings.

It shall be like people, like priest. As the great Bishop, Father, and Doctor of the Church, St John Chrysostom teaches:

> *Do you wish to know if the people of any place are righteous? Look what sort of a pastor they have. If you find him pious, just, a man of integrity, believe that the people fed by him will be the same, for they are seasoned with the salt of his wisdom.*

Do you wish to know if the people of any place are righteous? Look what sort of a pastor they have: it shall be like people, like priest.

And given that it shall be like people, like priest, and given that our culture is rotten to the core, what does that tell us about the sort of pastors that we've had, for the most part?

Speaking to you seminarians: it shall be like people, like priest. Do not fall into the trap of thinking you can say your office and your Mass and hear a few confessions and you're "good to go".

No, you are not: you may be "good to go" to hell.

You are preparing for pastoral ministry. That means you are preparing to take care of the Lord's sheep. Do not forget this.

You are preparing to work hard, very hard, and you are not preparing to lead a contemplative life. You are not preparing to be a bunch of professors of this or that. You are not preparing to build yourself some sort of comfortable little nest so that you can lead a life of leisure. You are preparing to take care of souls. A lot of those souls will be very broken and needy, and given the social conditions, it's only going to get worse and worse. You are preparing to take care of them. You are preparing to be pastors of souls. Do not forget this! The Word of God tells us that it shall be like people, like priest.

You are preparing to work with the wounded and broken sheep of the Lord. And the chances are that each one of you is at least somewhat wounded himself; a good number of our priests are wounded – some very wounded – and some are even broken.

But *nemo dat quod non habet* – no one can give what he does not have. If a priest is wounded himself (and in fact to the very degree he is wounded), he is not able to give his flock what they really need; he is not able to give them the truth and especially the charity they so desperately need. He's just not able, since no one can give what he does not have.

The result is that the wounded or broken priest ends up wounding a lot of the very people he's been sent out to care for: it shall be like people, like priest. They're turning to their priest, looking for love, looking for charity, but he is not able to give them what they really need.

A lot of the souls you are preparing to care for will be very broken and needy, very wounded, and given the social conditions, it's only going to get worse. Assuming you want to be part of the solution, and not part of the problem, you need to start preparing yourself.

Today.

So I'm going to give you 2 very practical things that you each need to start doing.

First: you need to start praying for the wounded and broken sheep that Our Lord is going to entrust to you, starting today. You need to start praying for them now. That's first.

And second: if you are not healed, if you are not at least well on the path to healing and wholeness yourself, then you need to start working on that.

Today.

You have a particular responsibility to understand this so that you can help and teach others:

For the lips of the priests shall keep knowledge, and men shall seek the law at his mouth, for he is the angel of the Lord of hosts. (Malachi 2:7)

No one can give what he does not have. Start praying for the wounded and broken sheep that Our Lord is going to entrust to you, and start working on your healing.

Today.

Appendix

HEALING PRAYERS

Closing ourselves:

I close myself to anything that is not of the Holy Spirit, and I open myself completely to Heaven.

To identify a wound:

Come Holy Spirit, help me to see myself as You see me – and to love myself as You love me. Blessed Mother, help me to see myself as You see me – and to love myself as You love me.

Act of the will:

Once we have identified a wound, we make an act of the will that we really want this to be healed and that we are willing to suffer whatever it takes to that end.

Renunciation:

I completely and utterly reject, with the full force of my will, anything and everything disordered or displeasing to God in my thoughts, attitudes and emotions concerning -------. I do this in the Holy Names of Jesus and Mary and in the Name of the Father and the Son and the Holy Spirit. Amen. (3x)

Prayers of Healing:

Blessed Mother, I beg you to come into this wound and wash, cleanse and purify it with your tears and the Precious Blood.

I beg You in Your Holy and Glorious Name, Jesus, and your Holy and Glorious name, Mary, to heal and reorder whatever is disordered or displeasing to God in this wound (wounded area, etc.)

I beg You in Your Holy and Glorious Name, Jesus, and your Holy and Glorious name, Mary, to fill this wound with charity, ----, and any other necessary or useful virtue.

Consecration:

Jesus and Mary, I consecrate this wound to You and I beg You in Your Holy and Glorious Name, Jesus, and your Holy and Glorious name, Mary, to stay and rule.

Appendix

NOTES

NOTES

Appendix

NOTES

NOTES

Appendix

NOTES

NOTES

Appendix

NOTES

NOTES

www.ingramcontent.com/pod-product-compliance
Lightning Source LLC
LaVergne TN
LVHW090952080826
845145LV00003B/984

* 9 7 8 1 7 3 2 8 0 2 9 2 6 *